COLORADO CABINS COTTAGES & LODGES

by

Hilton and Jenny Fitt-Peaster

Rocky Mountain Vacation Publishing, Inc.
Boulder, Colorado 80303-2799

Cover photo of McGregor Mountain Lodge's Iris Cottage,
Estes Park, Colorado, with Sundance Mountain in the background,
copyright © by Jim Osterberg, Brochures Plus, Estes Park, Colorado.
Back cover photos (top to bottom): a cabin at The Hideout, Glenwood Springs,
Colorado copyright © by Hilton Fitt-Peaster; the lodge at Wit's End, Bayfield,
Colorado, copyright © by Paul Myers, Omega Color Graphics, Durango,
Colorado; a cottage at Sundance Cottages, Estes Park, Colorado, copyright
© by Jim Osterberg, Brochures Plus, Estes Park, Colorado.

Cover design by Robert L. Schram, BookEnds, Boulder, Colorado.

Library of Congress Catalog Card Number: 93-83208

Publisher's Cataloging in Publication
(Prepared by Quality Books, Inc.)

Fitt-Peaster, Hilton.
    Colorado cabins, cottages & lodges : discover scenic vacation hideaways / Hilton &
Jenny Fitt-Peaster.
    p. cm.
    Includes index.
    ISBN 1-883087-00-7
    1. Hotels, taverns, etc.--Colorado--Guidebooks. 2. Vacation homes--Colorado--
Guidebooks. 3. Colorado--Description and travel--1981--Guidebooks. I. Fitt-Peaster,
Jenny. II. Title. III. Title: Colorado cabins, cottages and lodges.

TX907.3.C5F588 1993   647'.94788
                                                         QBI93-643

This publication is a directory intended to provide information only, not recommendations, war-
ranties, guarantees, inducements or endorsements of any kind. The information contained herein
was supplied by the individual businesses. Although the publisher has prepared this directory with
the information available as of April 10, 1993, it does not assume any responsibility, and expressly
disclaims any liability, for inaccuracies or errors regarding the information contained herein. Readers
are advised that prices and services are subject to change. The publisher would appreciate notice that
any information contained herein is no longer accurate.

Printed in the United States of America

10 9 8 7 6 5 4 3 2

This book is dedicated to all the many warm, wonderful people throughout Colorado who dedicate their lives to providing worthwhile vacations to the public at their cabins, cottages and lodges.

FOREWORD

This one-of-a-kind book offers answers to your questions about Colorado's abundant cabins, cottages, and lodges. In its pages, you'll find that romantic cabin getaway, the perfect family reunion cottage or a remote trout stream lodge.

I've known the authors, Hilton and Jenny Fitt-Peaster, for 10 years, and can assure you that no two people have traveled as many miles in this state seeking these sometimes hidden treasures. Hilton and Jenny have done all the work for you!

You'll find activities such as hiking, mountain biking, cross-country skiing, whitewater rafting, fly fishing, canoeing, hot air ballooning and more in fabulous locations throughout the state — many available right on the premises. The accommodations in this guidebook range from rustic to opulent, timberline to trailhead, historic to modern — all easily accessible to remote wilderness. Your dining options range from cozy kitchenettes to hearty family-style ranch fare to spectacular gourmet meals. The possibilities are endless!

I invite you to select a cabin, cottage or lodge and discover all Colorado has to offer. Let your adventure begin!

RICH MEREDITH
Executive Director
Colorado Tourism Board
April 1993

PREFACE

Colorado — an outdoor paradise. So much to see: splendorous mountains, wilderness areas, backcountry, wide open spaces, national parks, wild animals, ghost towns. So much to do: hiking, climbing, mountain biking, fishing, four-wheeling, boating, hunting, skiing, camping. You name it, we've got it.

But where do you stay to escape the ordinary and truly live the Colorado experience? Surely there are places off the beaten path that offer diverse, pleasant and unique adventures, yet close enough to enjoy vacation activities?

We know where they are — as executive directors of the Colorado Association of Campgrounds, Cabins and Lodges since 1977, we drive over 8,000 miles each year on Colorado's highways and back roads searching for and visiting owners and operators of Colorado's cabins, cottages and mountain lodges, often in remote places that typical travelers won't see when driving through.

Over the years, we've heard frequently from lodge owners and tourists alike. Lodge owners are anxious to tell vacationers what they have to offer, and vacationers are anxious to find them. Although we publish abbreviated write-ups on each place in our annual, free *Colorado Directory of Cabins, Lodges, Camping and Fun Things to Do*, tourists are hungry for more detail.

As a result, we've written the first definitive guide to Colorado's cabins, cottages and mountain lodges that are extremely enjoyable to visit and explore. On the following pages, you'll see that these places provide charming, alternative accommodations, from rustic to upscale, in the Rocky Mountain region at any season of the year.

The 230 accommodations listed are in alphabetical order by area name, and include detailed descriptions and easy-to-follow directions for your convenience. When making a decision on where to stay, remember that some of the best cottages, cabins and lodges are inexpensive. Also be aware that reservations are almost always required, sometimes months in advance, especially during peak season.

Consider a fall, winter or spring vacations when rates can be lower, reservations easier, things are quieter and the scenery even more spectacular.

None of the properties paid to be listed in this book. All of them are professional members of the Colorado Association of Campgrounds, Cabins & Lodges.

We hope you find this book enjoyable, useful and rewarding. Feel free to give us any feedback or comments about this book — and be sure to tell the cabin, cottage and lodge owners listed that you heard about them here.

We wish to acknowledge the invaluable services of the following people, without whom this book would have never been published: Rebekah Fitt-Peaster served as our Associate Publisher from day one. Early on, we retained Ben McDonald of Conifer, Colorado as a publisher's consultant; his advice and continuing guidance has proved helpful beyond measure. Rodney Sauer of Pika Graphics in Louisville, Colorado was the book's managing editor and supplied expert computer typesetting. Bob Quam offered valuable editorial, research and computer layout consultation. Hilary Lane provided talented editing and rewriting, and Amy Westfeldt was our proofreader. Robert L. Schram of BookEnds in Boulder, Colorado designed and prepared the cover, using the front- and back-cover photographs taken by Jim Osterberg of Brochures Plus in Estes Park, Colorado and Paul Myers of Omega Color Graphics in Durango, Colorado.

Thanks. Enjoy Colorado!

HILTON AND JENNY FITT-PEASTER
Authors
April 1993

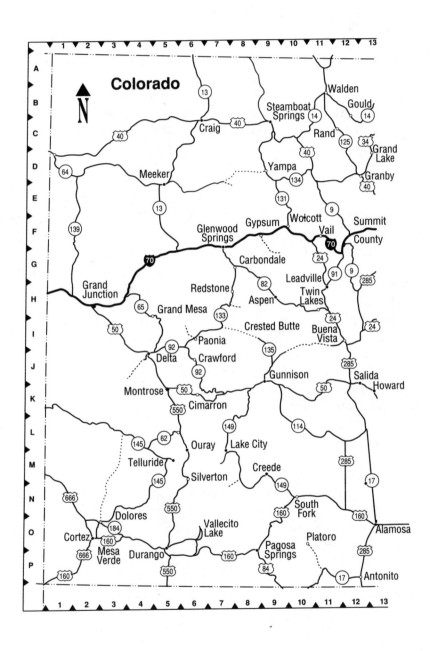

Map ix

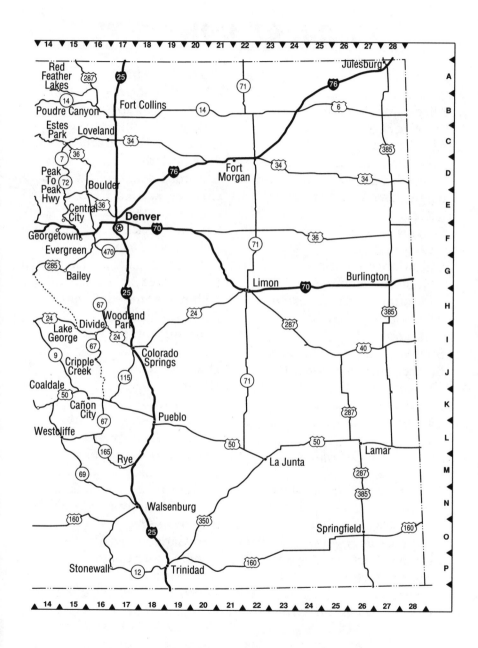

TABLE OF CONTENTS

INTRODUCTION

This book contains descriptions of a variety of cabins, lodges, cottages and fun things to do. The book is organized in a manner to make it easy for you to find accommodations in particular areas of Colorado. In the Table of Contents, locate town or area in which you are interested, then go to the page number listed for a description of the cabins and lodges in that area. Some towns are grouped together, so if you look up a particular town, you may find a cross reference directing you to the appropriate listing under a different heading. The town headings all include map coordinates; use these to help locate the town on the map at the front of this book. These map coordinates are the same as those shown on the official Colorado map. The town headings may also refer you to other nearby areas for additional listings.

Definitions

We realize you may not be familiar with all the terminology throughout these pages, so we've provided definitions here for your convenience.

Cabin, Cottage, Chalet, Guest House, or Vacation Home — what you call them often depends on where you're from. Cabins are often log or log-sided; cottages are frequently frame construction.

Housekeeping means equipped with a kitchenette, cooking and eating utensils.

Modern means a bathroom (toilet and hot shower or tub) are inside the cabin.

Rustic either describes atmosphere or style, or means a bathroom is *not* inside the cabin, but usually in another building.

Primitive means the premises does not have electricity.

Camper cabin means an inexpensive, non-housekeeping, rustic and sometimes primitive cabin. Bring your own sleeping bags or blankets. Camper cabins are usually not heated — think of them as a "wooden tent." They are usually located at a campground. A brand of camper cabin is a Kamping Kabin™, which is a trademark of Kampgrounds of America, Inc.

Lodge room, often called a historic hotel room, includes linens, a bathroom in the room or a shared bath down the hall. Rooms in a lodge are usually entered from inside the building.

Bed and breakfast room may be in a lodge, inn or owner's home, and always includes breakfast.

On-site trailer for rent means a travel trailer or small mobile home is set up on a campsite and may or may not include linens, cooking and eating utensils (inquire).

Camping available means campsites are available and suitable for family overnight camping in a tent or a recreation vehicle (RV). They usually have a fire ring or grill and picnic tables, and are accessible to nearby drinking water and modern restrooms, including hot showers.

Reservations, Facilities, and Fun Things To Do

When selecting places for your vacation, phone the owner or operator to check what they offer: price, facilities, reservation deposit/refund policy, pet policy, and so on.

Facilities at commercial campgrounds, cabin resorts and lodges often include a store with some groceries, ice, firewood, and camping and fishing supplies. They may also offer a game room, recreation hall, gifts and souvenirs, pool, hot tub, playground, basketball, volleyball, miniature golf and a snack bar or restaurant. Best of all, the owner/operator family lives on site to provide security and serve as your personal hosts.

Activities may include fishing, guides and outfitters, nature walks, hiking, hay rides, water sports, barbecue cookouts, potluck dinners, ice cream socials, campfire programs, movies, whitewater raft trips and kayaking, four wheeling, square dancing, sightseeing, tours, gold panning, rockhounding and horseback riding. In the fall, viewing the aspen colors and hunting are the most popular events. Winter brings snowmobiling, cross-country and downhill skiing, ice fishing, sleigh and snow-cat rides and snuggling up by a cozy fire. Inquire about rental equipment and instructions for wintertime activities. Season opening dates may change, depending on weather.

Altitude Awareness

In Colorado's high country, skies are bluer and stars are brighter because of our altitude. Our air is thinner, with less oxygen, than at sea level, especially above 8,000 feet, so until your body adjusts, go easy on physical activity; drink more water than usual; minimize your intake of alcohol, caffeine and salty foods; and eat high-carbohydrate foods, such as grains, fruits and vegetables. There is less atmosphere to screen out ultraviolet rays, so remember to use sunscreen and sunglasses. If you adopt the proper attitude toward Colorado's altitude, you and your family will have the most enjoyable vacation experience possible.

Rates

Cabin and room prices constantly change, both seasonally and annually, so instead of giving exact costs, we provide a price range. The **1993 rates** for two people per night are indicated this way:

$	=	**Under $25**
$$	=	**$25 – $40**
$$$	=	**$40 – $55**
$$$$	=	**$55 – $70**
$$$$$	=	**Over $70**

ALAMOSA

The city where the West meets the Southwest, Alamosa is surrounded by the majestic Sangre de Cristo and San Juan mountains and nestled along the Rio Grande River. Overlooking the San Luis Valley at about 7,500 feet, Alamosa boasts 360-plus days of sunshine. The nearby Great Sand Dunes National Monument is one of Colorado's most spectacular natural land formations. This "land of cool sunshine" abounds with easily accessible streams, lakes and hundreds of mountain trails for fishing, hunting and hiking enthusiasts.

Fun Things to Do

- Cattails Golf Course (719) 589-9515
- Fort Garland State Museum (719) 379-3512
- Great Sand Dunes Country Club (719) 378-2357
- Great Sand Dunes National Monument (719) 378-2313
- Luther E. Bean & E.S. Museums (719) 589-7151

Alamosa KOA & Kamping Kabins™

Bring your own sleeping bags and camping equipment to these rustic camper cabins that include an on-site swimming pool, game room and a laundromat.

You can fish within 2 miles, drive to the nearby Great Sand Dunes National Monument, or ride the Cumbres & Toltec Scenic Railroad within an hour. The Alamosa KOA is on the Navajo Trail to Mesa Verde and the Grand Canyon, and is just a short distance from historic old Ft. Garland.

Location: 3½ miles east of Alamosa and 20 miles west of Ft. Garland on Highway 160, near milepost 237.

3 camper cabins
Camping available
Rates: $

Yogi Chaudhry
6900 Juniper Lane (CB)
Alamosa CO 81101
(719) 589-9757

Pets: Yes
Elevation: 7,544
Credit Cards: VMD
Open April 1 to November 1

Great Sand Dunes Oasis & Camper Cabins

Enjoy a spectacular view of the Great Sand Dunes and the San Luis Valley from camper cabins, charming rental tepees or from tentsites nestled in piñon trees. Amenities include on-site hot showers, a laundromat, a recreation room, a grocery store and gift shops. A small cafe serves simple, but delicious meals. You can also fish in the scenic 300-acre facility's private pond without a license. In the fall, take an easy drive to excellent hunting in surrounding areas.

Reservations are required — ask about the special group rates. You may even bring your own horses.

Your hosts are happy to set up four-wheel drive tours into hard-to-reach areas of the Great Sand Dunes.

Location: At the entrance to the Great Sand Dunes National Monument, Highway 150, near milepost 16.

2 camper cabins
Camping available
Rates: $

Jim & Joyce Kuenkel, Owners
Mike & Patti Vittoria, Managers
5400 Highway 150 North (CB)
Mosca CO 81146
(719) 378-2222

Pets: Yes
Elevation: 8,000
Credit Cards: VM
Open April 1 to October 31

Allenspark: see Peak-to-Peak Scenic Highway Area. Map: D-14

Almont: see Gunnison. Map: J-9

ANTONITO

Includes Platoro. Map: P-13

When the first train pulled into Antonito in 1880, the town had been the traditional hub of commerce for the southern San Luis Valley. It lies between the Conejos and the San Antonio rivers at an elevation of 7,888 feet above sea level and is the gateway to the beautiful Conejos River canyon. This city was once the "mainline" of the infant Denver and Rio Grande rivers that traveled to the ancient capital of New Mexico and Santa Fe. Today, Antonito is the main station for the historic Cumbres & Toltec Scenic Railroad. The Conejos River offers excellent trout fishing.

Fun Things to Do

- Cumbres & Toltec Scenic Railroad (719) 376-5483
- End of the Rail Clydesdale Rides & Gifts (303) 376-2042
- First Crossing Restaurant (800) 323-9469, (719) 376-5441

Conejos Cabins & Gold Pan Acres Campground

Near the Continental Divide, these cabins have fireplaces with furnished wood, dishes, cooking utensils and bedding. You can cook your daily meals outside on the handy grills.

Plan to rent fishing boats to cruise the nearby Conejos River and the Platoro Reservoir or ride horseback to fish in the high lakes surrounding the area.

Location: Take Highway 17 west from Antonito 20 miles, near milepost 17. Go north 23 miles on gravel road.

11 housekeeping cabins
Camping available
Rates: $$$$

Lee & Phyllis Pennington
P.O. Box 8 (CB)
Antonito CO 81120-008
(719) 376-2547
November to April: (303) 483-7451

Pets: Yes (one pet per cabin)
Elevation: 9,750
Credit Cards: VM
Open May 15 to October 1

Cottonwood Meadows Cabins & Fly Shop

This is the San Luis Valley fly-fishing headquarters. The modern housekeeping cabins are comfortably equipped with a kitchenette, cooking and eating utensils and baths with a tub or shower. The guided fishing trips into the Rio Grande National Forest include the Conejos River and its many tributaries. Or, if you crave solitude, you can fish all day in the backwoods streams. Most trips are limited to no more than two guests per guide. The completely stocked fly shop has all you need, including rods, reels and waders. Buy your other supplies at the on-site grocery store.

In addition to guided fishing trips, you can arrange horseback riding and overnight trips into the wilderness. Other nearby attractions include the Cumbres & Toltec Scenic Railroad, the Great Sand Dunes National Monument and the Rio Grande Gorge.

Location: 5 miles west of Antonito on Highway 17, near milepost 35.

4 housekeeping cabins
Rates: Call for prices

Randy & Naomi Keys
34591 Highway 17 (CB)
Antonito CO 81120
(719) 376-5660

Pets: Yes
Elevation: 8,000
Credit Cards: VM
Open all year

FLY SHOP
Tackle-Cabins
Guide Service

Josey's Mogote Meadow

Situated on seven acres of grass and cottonwood trees, these modern housekeeping cabins come fully equipped with kitchenette, cooking and eating utensils and modern baths. In addition, there are on-site trailers for rent and 44 tent and RV hookup sites. All of these facilities offer a beautiful and relaxing atmosphere while you visit this scenic area. Enjoy nightly campfires, potluck dinners and Sunday pancake breakfasts.

Reservations are necessary.

Your hosts can arrange fishing tours on the beautiful Conejos River and nearby lakes. Josey's is conveniently located for easy day trips to the Great Sand Dunes National Monument, the Cumbres & Toltec Scenic Railroad, Red River, Taos and Chama, New Mexico and Wolf Creek Pass.

Location: 5 miles west of Antonito on Highway 17, near milepost 34.

2 housekeeping cabins
2 trailers for rent
Camping available
Rates: $$

Bob & Anne Josey
34127 Highway 17 (CB)
Antonito CO 81120
(719) 376-5774
November to April: (505) 268-0925

Pets: Yes
Elevation: 8,066
Credit Cards: No
Open May 1 to October 15

Twin Rivers Cabins & RV Park

Located at the mouth of the beautiful Conejos Canyon, this area sports excellent fishing and hunting. You can walk out your back door and cast your reel into the two privately stocked streams, or fish in nearby reservoirs, mountain lakes, rivers and streams. The newly remodeled, country-decorated housekeeping cabins, hidden away in the tree-lined meadow, all have full kitchens, linens, dishes, utensils and color television. For variety, you can participate in nightly campfires, visit the large, screened pavilion, take your kids to the on-site playground and eat a complimentary Sunday morning pancake breakfast. Twin Rivers also offers campsites with full hookups and shaded tentsites. Stock up in the nearby tackle and gift shop.

Take many scenic drives throughout the Rio Grande National Forest and along the spectacular border of Colorado and New Mexico. Ride the famous Cumbres & Toltec Scenic Railroad or visit the scenic Monte Vista Wildlife Refuge.

Location: 5 miles west of Antonito and the Cumbres & Toltec Scenic Railroad depot, on Highway 17, near milepost 34.

8 housekeeping cabins
Camping available
Rates: $$

Barbara Jordan
34044 Highway 17 (CB)
Antonito CO 81120
(719) 376-5710

Pets: Yes
Elevation: 8,066
Credit Cards: D
Open May 1 to November 15

BAILEY

Also see Denver Area and Evergreen. Map: G-15

Located in Park County, Bailey is just 45 miles southwest of Denver and is surrounded by the Pike National Forest. It is an undiscovered mountain hideaway, yet near the big city of Denver. At an altitude of 7,750 feet, it is an excellent area for hunting and fishing.

Fun Things to Do

- Bailey Park County Historical Society Museum (303) 838-7253 or (303) 674-9713
- McGraw Historical Park (303) 838-9511
- South Park Historical City Museum, Fairplay (719) 836-2387

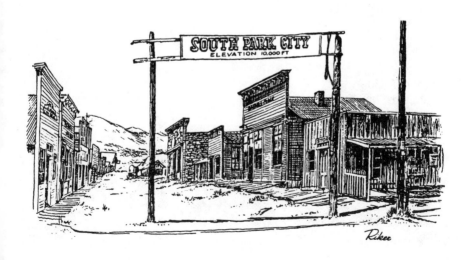

Glen Isle Resort Lodge & Cabins

This national historic site on the Platte River offers activities all year round. You will be "roughing it" in well-insulated, well-furnished cabins that sleep up to 10 people. All cabins contain fully equipped kitchens, private baths, easy chairs, bedding and linens, fireplaces (wood provided) and gas heat. The lodge, built in 1900, is listed on the National Register of Historic Sites and has been owned by the same family for more than 50 years. Decorated with antiques, the lodge offers a dining room and gift and antique shops. The Glen Isle Resort Lodge and Cabins provides a restful, informal and reasonably priced family retreat.

You may rent the lodge rooms with or without breakfast.

Activities include a children's playground, fishing, hiking, horseback riding, games, picnics, cookouts, sing-a-longs, square dancing, movies, chuck wagon dinners, library, bird watching and hunting. In the winter, you can partake in sledding, ice skating and skiing. Located centrally in Colorado, you can reach practically any point of interest by car.

Location: 50 miles southwest of Denver on Highway 285, near milepost 221.

13 housekeeping cabins
12 lodge rooms
Rates: $$$ to $$$$

Gordon & Barbara Tripp
P.O. Box 128 (CB)
Bailey CO 80421
(303) 838-5461

Pets: Yes
Elevation: 7,830
Credit Cards: No
Open all year

Bayfield: see Vallecito Lake Area. Map: P-6

Bellvue: see Poudre River Canyon Area. Map: B-14

Black Canyon of the Gunnison National Monument: see Cimarron, Crawford, Delta and Montrose. Map: K-5

BOULDER

Also see Peak-to-Peak Scenic Highway Area. Map: D-16

When you first see Boulder, you notice the beautiful setting — the Rocky Mountains dramatically rise to the west and the plains stretch endlessly to the east. Often called "Camelot," Boulder sports a pleasant year-round climate, diverse restaurants, an exciting university environment and an intimate, charming small-town atmosphere. Ideally located between Denver and Rocky Mountain National Park, there are endless activities and cultural events during any season — you can ski nearby slopes, hike miles of trails, shop the renovated Downtown Pedestrian Mall, tour turn-of-the-century homes, visit the University of Colorado or explore nearby historic mining towns, to name just a few.

Fun Things to Do

- Boulder Historical Society & Museum (303) 449-3464
- Coal Creek Golf Course, Louisville (303) 666-7888
- Flatirons Golf Course (303) 442-7851
- Lake Valley Golf Course (303) 719-444-2114
- Leanin' Tree Museum of Western Art (303) 530-1442
- University of Colorado Arts Galleries (303) 492-6165
- University of Colorado Heritage Center (303) 492-6329
- University of Colorado Museum (303) 492-6165

The Alps Boulder Canyon Inn

The Alps is a historic luxury country inn located 2 miles from downtown Boulder in scenic Boulder Canyon. The 12 elegant guest rooms are furnished with period antiques and include luxurious bathrooms and Victorian fireplaces. Several rooms feature double whirlpool tubs — two even have old-fashioned, claw-foot tubs. The inn serves gourmet breakfasts, afternoon teas and nightly desserts.

The Alps Boulder Canyon Inn is located at the very edge of the Front Range of the Rocky Mountains. Head down the canyon to Boulder or Denver for shopping, cultural events and sight-seeing year round. Take a leisurely drive up the canyon to view the snow-capped peaks of the great divide, visit old mining towns, drive the Peak-to-Peak Scenic Highway, or hike to high mountain passes, glaciers and lakes. Or, if you want to relax, fish in Boulder Creek and bask in the scenic beauty of the high canyon walls.

Location: Highway 119, near milepost 38.

12 lodge rooms
Rates: $$$$$

John & Jeannine Vanderhart
P.O. Box 18298 (CB)
Boulder CO 80308-8298
(303) 444-5445

Pets: No
Elevation: 5,700
Credit Cards: VMAD
Open all year

Boulder Mountain Lodge

Wouldn't you like to be in the mountains and yet just five minutes away from the charming university town of Boulder? This lodge is nestled against the mountains, with Four Mile Creek flowing through the property. You can stay in rooms with or without kitchenettes, or in tentsites and full hookup campsites. Relax in the swimming pool or, after a hard day of mountain exercise, soak in the hot tub.

By driving up Four Mile Canyon or Boulder Canyon, you can explore old mining towns, hike beautiful trails and see spectacular vistas. In the winter, try downhill and cross-country skiing in surrounding areas. Visit the University of Colorado Boulder campus, historic Chautauqua Park, the National Institute of Standards and Technology, the National Center for Atmospheric Research, Boulder Falls and historic mining towns, including the working gold mine at Caribou, west of Nederland in Boulder County.

Location: West on Highway 119 to Four Mile Canyon (4 miles from the mouth of Boulder Canyon), near milepost 39.

18 motel rooms with kitchenette
4 motel rooms without kitchenette
Camping available
Rates: $$ to $$$$$

Bob & Bret Gibson
91 Four Mile Canyon Rd. (CB)
Boulder CO 80302
(303) 444-0882

Pets: Yes
Elevation: 5,600
Credit Cards: VMA
Open all year

Breckenridge: see Summit County. Map: G-12

BUENA VISTA

This small town is nestled at the base of the Collegiate and Sawatch Mountain Ranges on the banks of the Arkansas River. Buena Vista is noted for its hospitable people, home-town atmosphere and healthy environment. It's a place where people take pride in their community and maintain a serene, yet spirited lifestyle. Winter and summer sports abound in the dry, mild climate. Nearby mountains offer skiing, snowmobiling, fishing, white-water rafting and natural hot springs.

Fun Things to Do

- Buena Vista Heritage Museum (719) 395-8458
- Buffalo Joe River Trips (719) 395-8757 or (800) 356-7984
- Collegiate Peaks Golf Course (719) 395-8189
- Cottonwood Hot Springs (800) 241-4119, (719) 395-6434
- Mt. Princeton Hot Springs, Nathrop (719) 395-2361
- River Runners Ltd. (800) 525-2081

Bar VV Cabins & Campground

Enjoy a quick getaway or spend your whole summer vacation in this mountain retreat, nestled among the 14,000-foot Collegiate Peaks. The rustic mountain cabins are clean and comfortable. Some of the authentic log cabins have kitchenettes to satisfy your mountain-sized appetite, or you can use the outdoor grill and tables for a barbecue. Build one of those great evening campfires you've always dreamed about with the free, abundant firewood.

The beautiful Collegiate Peaks offer a great variety of mountain recreation. Take secluded walks in the woods from great trailheads, or climb one of the nearby 14,000-foot peaks. The Arkansas River valley offers fishing, hiking, walking and rafting in the wilderness. Visit the charming mountain towns of Leadville, Buena Vista and Salida during the summer to see Rodeo Days, burro races, kayak races and quaint mining town architecture.

Location: 14 miles north of Buena Vista, 17 miles south of Leadville on Highway 24, near milepost 197.

3 housekeeping cabins
2 non-housekeeping cabins
Camping available
Rates: $$ to $$$

Dave & Nancy Van Der Hoop
40671 Highway 24 (CB)
Buena Vista CO 81211
(719) 395-2338

Pets: Yes (with deposit)
Elevation: 9,000
Credit Cards: No
Open May 1 to September 30

Buena Vista Family Resort & Campground

This is a destination campground that has camper cabins for those who enjoy the great outdoors, but don't want the work of setting up a tent. Groups can view some of the highest peaks in Colorado from the pavilion. Buena Vista Family Campground & Resort has a small cook-shack that offers breakfast and dinner, including buffalo burger cookouts, ice cream socials and other events over the summer.

Buena Vista Family Campground & Resort has weekly, monthly, seasonal and group rates. If you like to travel with your horses, be sure to make a reservation for them at the "horse motel."

Experience the flavor of the West with hayrack rides, trail rides, gold panning and rock hunting. Enjoy horseback riding, hiking, trekking through ghost towns and four-wheel jeeping in the Sawatch Mountain Range. The Arkansas River provides excellent water sports, including rafting, kayaking and fishing. If you like golfing, visit the nearby nine-hole golf course.

Location: Centrally located on Highway 285/24, near milepost 214, 4 miles southeast of Buena Vista and ¾ miles east of Johnson Village.

4 camper cabins
Camping available
Rates: $

Mike & Ruth Simpson
27700 Country Rd. 303 (CB)
Buena Vista CO 81211
(719) 395-8318
(800) 621-9960
Fax: (719) 395-2192

Pets: Yes
Elevation: 8,000
Credit Cards: VM
Open all year

Cottonwood Hot Springs Inn & Cabins

Home of the Jump Steady Restaurant, the Cottonwood Hot Springs Inn is nestled in a high-mountain valley of the Majestic Collegiate Peaks Range, bordered by Cottonwood Creek and surrounded by the San Isabel National Forest. Rent one of three rustic creekside log cabins with kitchenettes and spacious guest rooms, or stay in one of the tepee campsites or bunkhouses. Work out in the exercise room and relax in the private hot mineral springs spa afterwards. An on-site restaurant features delicious, nutritious meals in a spacious dining room with a cozy fireside conversation area. There are no televisions or phones in the rooms or cabins; great for group retreats.

Reservations are recommended, especially for the special group, weekly and monthly rates — children under three stay free. Your hosts are happy to take reservations from your travel agent.

Enjoy hiking in the nearby areas of Cottonwood Creek and Collegiate Peaks. There's also fishing, hunting, skiing, snowmobiling close by — something for everyone during any season.

Location: 5½ miles west of Buena Vista on Highway 306, near milepost 5; 9 miles from the Continental Divide.

3 housekeeping cabins
12 lodge rooms
Rates: $$$

Cathy Manning & Dian Lee Key
8999 County Road 306 (CB)
Buena Vista CO 81211
(800) 241-4119
(719) 395-6434

Pets: Yes (with deposit)
Elevation: 8,500
Credit Cards: VMD
Open all year

Love Ranch

The Love Ranch was named during the 1930s when Mark and Josephine Love purchased a ranch in Chalk Creek Canyon, a mountain paradise located between Mount Antero and Mount Princeton. Now a guest ranch, this resort is a friendly, family kind of place with its modern and rustic cabins adjacent to numerous streams.

You'll find plenty of fishing close by in the ranch trout stream and in the two trout lakes just a mile from the cabins. Some nearby activities include horseback riding, hiking to mountain lakes, swimming in the Princeton Hot Springs pools, visiting ghost towns and whitewater rafting. Visit the town of Buena Vista for golfing and fine dining.

Location: 6 miles south of Buena Vista on Highway 285, near milepost 142, then 8 miles west on County Road 162.

9 housekeeping cabins
Rates: $ to $$$$

Don & Sharon Putnam
18670 County Rd. 162 (CB)
Nathrop CO 81236
(719) 395-2366
Winter: (419) 529-6926

Pets: Yes
Elevation: 8,500
Credit Cards: VM
Open April 15 to December 15

Rainbow Lake Resort

These clean and cozy cabins, with fully equipped kitchenettes, are set on a picturesque, stocked lake. This mountain paradise is located just below 14,192-foot Mt. Yale in the Collegiate Peak Range.

Reservations are required.

Participate in the best stream fishing, sightseeing, hiking, hunting and backpacking in Colorado. The nearby Colorado Trail offers a unique look into this area.

Location: 8 miles west of Buena Vista on Highway 306, near milepost 8.

18 housekeeping cabins
Rates: $$$

Russell & Pat Coffey
21509 County Rd. 306
P.O. Box 666 (CB)
Buena Vista CO 81211-0666
(719) 395-2509
Off-season: (405) 643-5380

Pets: No
Elevation: 9,300
Credit Cards: VM
Open May 1 to October 1

Sagewood Cabins

High in the heart of the Collegiate Peaks Range, Sagewood Cabins are quaint, quiet, country log cabins located on a small family ranch. A true Colorado getaway, the cabins, adjacent to the San Isabel National Forest, have no televisions or phones (the office phone is available if you need it). Some cabins have fireplaces; all have private baths and lofts. Each is set up for basic housekeeping with dishes, cooking utensils and linens.

You're centrally located in an area with hiking, fishing, horseback riding, jeep trails, ghost towns, snowmobiling, skiing, shopping or resting, relaxing and enjoying life away from it all. Stay for a night, a week or a month.

Location: 11½ miles north of Buena Vista on Highway 24, near milepost 199/200, ¼ mile west of the highway.

3 housekeeping cabins
Rates: $$$

Kristen Ahlstedt
38951-B North Highway 24 (CB)
Buena Vista CO 81211
(719) 395-2582

Pets: Yes (with small fee and prior approval)
Elevation: 9,000
Credit Cards: No
Open May 1 to November 1 (later by reservation)

Thunder Lodge

Eight roomy log cabins are nestled along the tree-lined banks of Cottonwood Creek. All cabins come with modern conveniences, such as fully equipped kitchens and color cable television, yet they retain a Western Indian motif through pine and oak interiors and furnishings.

The lodge is open all year, with off-season rates. Cribs are available at no extra charge; children three and under stay free. The lodge requires a one-night deposit with reservations.

A wide range of year-round activities are available, including sightseeing, trout fishing, hiking, downhill and cross-country skiing, snowmobiling on groomed trails, hunting and just plain relaxing.

Location: 2 blocks north of the stoplight and 1 block west of Highway 24, near milepost 210 in Buena Vista.

8 housekeeping cabins
Rates: $$$

Robert Reichert
207 Brookdale Ave.
P.O. Box 504 (CB)
Buena Vista CO 81211-0504
(719) 395-2245

Pets: Yes
Elevation: 7,900
Credit Cards: VMD
Open all year

Woodland Brook Cabins

These cabins offer mountain seclusion with in-town convenience. Set off of the highway in a cottonwood and Ponderosa pine grove, Woodland Brook is quiet and relaxing. Cabins have fully equipped kitchens; some have fireplaces and cable television. A new, bubbly hot tub is wonderful after a day of mountain adventuring.

Fish the lakes and streams of this pleasant valley, or visit historic ghost towns and mines. The cabins are a good base camp for winter skiing at Monarch and Cooper ski areas, both only 45 minutes away. The area also features snowmobiling and cross-country skiing.

Location: Within city limits, a few blocks off of Highway 24, near milepost 210.

13 housekeeping cabins
Rates: $$ to $$$

Carl & Debra Sapp
226 S San Juan
P.O. Box 418 (CB)
Buena Vista CO 81211-0418
(719) 395-2922

Pets: Yes
Elevation: 7,900
Credit Cards: VMD
Open all year

CAÑON CITY

Also see Coaldale. Map: K-19

Considered the climate capital of Colorado, Cañon City's natural setting protects it from harsh weather. The Arkansas River flows through the city, forming one of the most spectacular attractions in the state — the Royal Gorge. The world's highest suspension bridge hangs a dizzying 1,053 feet above the rushing Arkansas River, offering unforgettable vistas. The area touts exciting rafting, fishing and hiking. And, the Colorado Territorial Prison, built in 1868, is the only prison museum located next to a currently operating prison.

Fun Things to Do

- Buckskin Joe Park & Railway (719) 275-5149 or (719) 275-5485
- Buffalo Joe River Trips (719) 395-8757 or (800) 356-7984
- Cañon City Fine Arts Center (719) 275-2790
- Cañon City Municipal Museum & Rudd House (719) 269-9018
- Colorado Territorial Prison Museum & Park (719) 269-3015
- Echo Canyon River Expeditions, Inc. (800) 748-2953
- Indian Springs Ranch National Natural Landmark (719) 372-3907
- River Runners Ltd. (800) 525-2081
- Royal Gorge Bridge Park (719) 275-7507
- Royal Gorge Scenic Railway (719) 275-5485
- Shadow Hills Golf Course (719) 275-0603

Royal View Camper Cabins & Campground

These well-equipped camper cabins offer a spectacular view of the Royal Gorge Bridge. Two of the cabins have two sets of bunk beds; the third has one bunk bed and one double bed. Each cabin has a picnic table and grill close to the showers and restrooms. The campground has all the facilities to make your vacation worry-free — an on-site store, club room, swimming pool, game room, a miniature golf course, volleyball, basketball and a laundromat

Your hosts can help arrange full- and half-day whitewater raft trips on the Arkansas River. In the evening, you can watch one of the nightly movies, while during the day, you can tour nearby Royal Gorge, Cripple Creek, the Garden Park Fossil area and the Colorado Territorial Prison Museum, or go horseback riding to one of the many scenic areas.

Location: On Highway 50, near milepost 269, 1 mile west of Royal Gorge Exit (south side).

3 camper cabins
Camping available
Rates: $ (no charge for 3rd and 4th persons)

Joe & Myrtle Manning
0227 8-Mile Hill (CB)
Cañon City CO 81212
(719) 275-1900

Pets: Yes
Elevation: 6,000
Credit Cards: VMD
Open April 1 to November 15

Yogi Bear's Jellystone Park Camp-Resort

Come visit Yogi on 23 pine-covered acres, in view of the Royal Gorge Bridge. These camper cabins are a comfortable and inexpensive way to enjoy the Royal Gorge area. The camp-resort serves pancake breakfasts to start off your day with energy. They also have a grocery store, clean showers, two playgrounds and volleyball and basketball courts. Relax after a day of exploring the mountains in the swimming pool or hot tub, or build a cozy fire in your camper cabin with the provided firewood.

Enjoy the on-site entertainment, including nightly movies, morning cartoons and hayrides with Yogi.

Location: 9 miles west of Cañon City, on Highway 50, near milepost 269, at the junction of Colorado Highway 9.

2 camper cabins
2 trailers for rent
Camping available
Rates: $$

Dennis & Ellen Burcham
43595 Highway 50
P.O. Box 1025 (CB)
Cañon City CO 81212-1025
(719) 275-2128

Pets: Yes
Elevation: 6,350
Credit Cards: VMD
Open all year

CARBONDALE

Also see Redstone-Marble Area. Map: G-8

Mount Sopris dominates the vista of this charming town in the Crystal River Valley. The rugged beauty of the area provides the perfect setting for a myriad of activities, including visiting art galleries, fine restaurants and craft shows. Carbondale also has year-round outdoor sports and recreation. Located between Aspen and Glenwood Springs, this valley offers unique charm and secluded, untouched scenic beauty.

Fun Things to Do

- Mount Sopris Historical Society Museum (303) 963-2889
- Spring Gulch Cross-Country Ski Center (303) 963-1890

B-R-B Crystal River Resort

Rocky Mountain splendor at its finest! B-R-B, located at the base of Mount Sopris on the beautiful Crystal River, offers tranquil mountain beauty, coupled with unique and comfortable facilities. The main lodge has a game room, small grocery store and gift shop. Modern log cabins, equipped with kitchens and linens, accommodate up to 10 people. Each cabin has its own fire pit, picnic table and barbecue grill. An open-air hot tub behind the main lodge is a welcome retreat after a day of adventuring.

Rafting trips, jeep tours and horseback riding are minutes away. Local fishing and hunting are some of the best in the country. Tour historic sites in Marble, Redstone and much more.

Location: On Highway 133, near milepost 62, 6 miles south of Carbondale.

13 housekeeping cabins
Camping available
Rates: $$$$ to $$$$$

Dick & Maryanne Fedderman
7202 Highway 133 (CB)
Carbondale CO 81623
(303) 963-2341

Pets: Yes, with deposit
Elevation: 6,200
Credit Cards: VM
Open all year

Harmony House Bed & Breakfast

The owners invite you to share their lovely log home situated on a tree-covered acre near the confluence of the Crystal and Roaring Fork rivers. Their house grew from a one-room cabin to a rambling, five-bedroom log home, with halls, greenhouses, lofts, dens and assorted nooks and crannies where adults can hide from the kids and vice versa. The accommodations include a guest room with shared bath and a housekeeping apartment cabin with a private bath. The hosts grow fruit, vegetables, flowers and honey in the summer and keep goats and chickens year round.

You must make reservations; no walk-ins.

Harmony House is near the famous Glenwood Springs and 30 minutes from the world-renowned Aspen/Snowmass area. You can rent mountain bikes and cross-country skis in Carbondale or charter airplane and helicopter rides at nearby airports.

Location: Take Highway 82 to Highway 133; turn west on Satank Road.

1 housekeeping cabin apartment
1 bed and breakfast room
Rates: room = $$$; apartment = $$$$

Jane Hendricks & Patrick Noel
0990 Satank Rd. (CB)
Carbondale CO 81623
(303) 963-3369

Pets: No
Elevation: 6,200
Credit Cards: No
Open all year

Cascade: see Colorado Springs Area. Map: I-17

Cedaredge: see Grand Mesa Area. Map: I-5

Central City: see Peak-to-Peak Scenic Highway Area. Map: M-28

Chimney Rock: see Pagosa Springs Area. Map: P-7

CIMARRON

Known for its old narrow-gauge railroad, Cimarron still maintains the train and part of the original trestle crossing over Cimarron Creek. In addition, you'll find the 469-foot Morrow Point Dam and Cimarron Canal, which supply water for the arid Uncompahgre Valley. Along with excellent fishing and camping, you can experience peace and quiet in the Uncompahgre National Forest.

Pleasant Valley Cabins & Campground

A good place to vacation and relax, Pleasant Valley Cabins & Campground is nestled in the Cimarron Valley of the Little Cimarron Stream. This wonderful family place is clean, quiet and friendly, with fireplaces and kitchenettes in some cabins, modern restrooms, hot showers, a coin laundromat, hunting and fishing licenses and a convenience store. You can also select from their wide variety of antiques and collectibles.

Reservations are accepted with a one-day deposit. Children and controlled pets are welcome.

On the premises or nearby, you can partake in excellent trout fishing, deer and elk hunting, jeeping and antique shopping. Many major attractions are also close by, including the Black Canyon of the Gunnison National Monument and Blue Mesa Reservoir.

Location: 3 miles east of Cimarron on Highway 50, near milepost 115.

5 housekeeping cabins
2 non-housekeeping cabins
Camping available
Rates: $$

Larry & Linda Griffin
84100 E. Highway 50
P.O. Box 127 (CB)
Cimarron CO 81220-0127
(303) 249-8330

Pets: Yes
Elevation: 7,500
Credit Cards: VMAD
Open May 1 to December 1

Clark: see Steamboat Springs Area. Map B-9

COALDALE

Map: K-14

Dating from 1871, Coaldale was an early stagecoach and railroad town. Settlers, noting the abundant native piñon pine, built coke kilns here. Ute Indians called this area "Pleasant Valley" because of the lush green valley that surrounds the area. Popular activities include river rafting and hiking.

Fun Things To Do

- Lazy J Rafting Company (800) 678-4274, (719) 942-4274

Lazy J Resort & Rafting Company

Enjoy a bit of the very best the West has to offer at Lazy J Resort & Rafting Company. The resort, situated on the banks of the Arkansas River, is known as the spectacular Grand Canyon of the Arkansas. The modern log cabins and motel rooms, some with kitchenettes and fireplaces, have beautiful views of the Sangre de Cristo Mountains. There is an on-site laundromat, gift shop and restaurant.

Lazy J sponsors both horseback riding and rafting trips. They specialize in full- or half-day raft trips, but the more adventurous can arrange overnight or custom journeys. You might want to try the "saddle and paddle" combination trip, which includes both horses and rafts. If you prefer river fishing, cast your line from the resort, or hike to one of the many nearby fishing areas.

Location: 30 miles west of the Royal Gorge on Highway 50, near milepost 242.

10 camper cabins
3 housekeeping cabins
1 motel room with kitchenette
4 motel rooms without kitchenette
3 trailers
Camping available
Rates: $$$

Jeff Jeffries
16373 Highway 50
P.O. Box 109 (CB)
Coaldale CO 81222
(719) 942-4274
(800) 678-4274

Pets: Yes
Elevation: 6,480
Credit Cards: VMAD
Open April 1 to December 1

Colorado National Monument: see Delta, Map: J-4 and Grand Mesa Area, Map: I-5

COLORADO SPRINGS AREA

Includes Cascade, Fountain, Green Mountain Falls,
Manitou Springs and Woodland Park. Map: I-17

Catch the excitement of Pikes Peak mountain majesty. From a morning ride on the Pikes Peak Cog Railway to the dramatic 14,110-foot summit, to the sunny charm of an afternoon hike through an alpine forest near Manitou Springs, the Colorado Springs area offers a myriad of activities. Visit the breathtaking natural red rock formations of the Garden of the Gods or tour the U.S. Air Force Academy. Fish for Rocky Mountain trout in the fresh, pine-scented air of this high-country region.

Fun Things to Do

- A.B. Jeep Tours (719) 593-9837
- Black Forest Observatory (719) 495-3828
- Broadmoor Golf Club (719) 577-5790
- Carriage House Museum (719) 632-7711 ext. 5353
- Cheyenne Mountain Zoological Park & Will Rogers Shrine of the Sun (719) 475-9555
- Colorado Springs Fine Arts Center (719) 634-5581
- Colorado Springs Pioneers' Museum (719) 578-6650
- Flying W Ranch (800) 232-FLYW or (719) 598-4000
- Ghost Town (719) 634-0696
- Hidden Inn Trading Post at Garden of the Gods (719) 632-2303
- May Natural History Museum (719) 576-0450
- Miramont Castle Museum, Manitou Springs (719) 685-1011
- Pikes Peak Auto Hill Climb Museum, Manitou Springs (719) 685-5996
- Rainbow Falls Trout Fishing and Horseback Riding (719) 687-9074
- Swiss Miss Shop (719) 684-9679 and (800) 521-GIFT
- Ute Pass Historical Society & Pikes Peak Museum, Woodland Park (303) 687-3041
- Valley Hi Golf Course (719) 578-6925
- Western Museum of Mining & Industry (719) 598-0880
- White House Ranch Historic Site (719) 578-6777
- World Figure Skating Hall of Fame & Museum (719) 635-5200

Becker's Lane Lodge

Relax in a quiet setting of towering elms and cottonwoods, located at the south entrance of the fascinating Garden of the Gods, with its red rock formations and mysterious "balanced rock." Rooms have fully equipped kitchenettes, private baths, color cable television and air-conditioning. Lodge facilities include coin laundromat, heated pool and barbecue area. During the summer, the lodge serves a delicious continental breakfast.

Pets are welcome; however, there are some restrictions and owners must adhere to guidelines.

You'll be close to historic downtown Manitou Springs, one of the most scenic towns in the Pikes Peak Region. You can also enjoy shopping and hunting for antiques around town. Nearby attractions include the Garden of the Gods, Cliff Dwellings, Cave of the Winds, the Pikes Peak Railway, the Air Force Academy and many museums.

Location: North of Manitou Avenue on Becker's Lane.

8 motel rooms with kitchenette
9 motel rooms without kitchenette
Rates: $$ to $$$

June Hummel & Laurie Larson
115 Beckers Lane (CB)
Manitou Springs CO 80829
(719) 685-1866

Pets: Yes
Elevation: 6,500
Credit Cards: VMA
Open all year

Buffalo Lodge Cottages

Built in the early 1900s, Buffalo Lodge is one of the historical landmarks of Colorado Springs. In the '20s and early '30s, it was ranked as one of the most modern lodges in the area and was a favorite place of Teddy Roosevelt and actress Linda Darnell. Located on four acres of tree-filled grounds, the main lodge still sports the antiques and furnishings of the era. The cabins are the original buildings, but they have been modernized and air-conditioned for comfort. A grassy area features a large play area for children, picnic tables, charcoal broilers, a swimming pool and hot tubs. Horseback riding stables are right next door.

The lodge is within walking distance of the Garden of the Gods, between historic Old Colorado Springs and Manitou Springs. And in just under an hour, you can drive to scenic Cripple Creek.

Location: Two blocks north of 3700 West Colorado Boulevard, off of Highway 24, near milepost 300.

17 housekeeping cottages
23 non-housekeeping cottages
Rates: $$ to $$$$$

Dennis & Donna Swanson
2 El Paso Blvd. (CB)
Colorado Springs CO 80904
(719) 634-2851
(800) 235-7416

Pets: Yes (deposit required)
Elevation: 6,000
Credit Cards: VMAD
Open May 24 to October 15

Colorado Springs South KOA & Kamping Kabins™

Enjoy a carefree vacation in the Colorado Springs area from these modern camper cabins. Return from a day's adventures to relax in the indoor swimming pool and hot tub, or take the kids to the game room and children's playground. An on-site store and laundromat allows you to spend more time playing and less time doing errands.

You can also join in campground activities, such as hayrides, nightly movies and the summer's weekend pancake breakfasts. The Colorado Springs South KOA is close to Pikes Peak, Fort Carson, the Air Force Academy, Cripple Creek casinos, the Garden of the Gods, the Cave of the Winds and the Royal Gorge.

Location: Highway I-25, exit 132.

6 camper cabins
Camping available
Rates: $$

Robert & Sandy Speight
8100 S. Bandley Drive (CB)
Fountain CO 80817
(719) 382-7575

Pets: Yes
Elevation: 5,546
Credit Cards: VMD
Open April 1 to November 1

Columbine Inn

Columbine Inn is a romantic, seven-room inn nestled in the mountains just 15 minutes outside Colorado Springs. The rooms feature private baths, queen-sized beds and outdoor decks. The restaurant serves lunch and dinner seven days a week and breakfast on weekends. There is also an outdoor deck to enjoy the mountain splendor while you dine.

Reservations are recommended, but not required.

The Inn is within walking distance of fishing, swimming, tennis, hiking, horseback riding, streams, parks and picnic areas. In the winter, enjoy nearby ice skating, sleigh-riding and skiing.

Location: Green Mountain Falls Exit off of Highway 24, near milepost 290.

7 lodge rooms
Rates: $$$$

Debbie Grant
10755 Ute Pass Ave.
P.O. Box 558 (CB)
Green Mountain Falls CO 80819
(719) 684-9063

Pets: No
Elevation: 7,800
Credit Cards: MVD
Open April to December

Dillon Motel Cabins

Within a mile of Manitou Springs, relax in these clean, air-conditioned cabins or swim in the large heated pool while enjoying a spectacular view of Pikes Peak. All cabins have cable color television and new king- and queen-sized beds. The cabins are designed in an old-West village theme — depending on your mood, you can stay in the bank, the Wells Fargo office, Mom's Cafe or the Sheriff's Office!

Reservations require one night's deposit or a valid credit card number. Check in after 2:00 p.m.; check out by 10:00 a.m.

An excellent place for vacationing, you'll be centrally located to most attractions within a mile of a major supermarket, laundromat and drugstore and within a short walk to restaurants and a convenience store. Manitou Springs offers wonderful shopping and dining in a beautiful historic downtown area. You can make bus reservations for Cripple Creek gambling at the office. Dillon Motel Cabins are centrally located to all Pikes Peak area attractions.

Location: Off of Highway 24, near milepost 299.

5 housekeeping cabins
12 non-housekeeping cabins
Rates: $ to $$$

George & Joanne James
134 Manitou Ave. (CB)
Manitou Springs CO 80829
(719) 685-5225

Pets: No
Elevation: 6,500
Credit Cards: VMAD
Open May 1 to October 1

El Colorado Lodge

Enjoy the tranquil beauty and adventure of the Pikes Peak Region in the family-owned and operated El Colorado Lodge, which features historic Southwest adobe-style modernized "casitas" that sleep from one to six people. All cabins have heat, air-conditioning, color cable television and telephones. Some cabins have kitchens, beamed ceilings and fireplaces. Other pleasant amenities include a huge swimming pool, a hospitality room, a pavilion, outdoor barbecue grills, a patio, picnic tables and a children's playground. This is a great place to have that family reunion this year!

El Colorado Lodge is centrally located for all Pikes Peak Region attractions and sights.

Location: Off of Highway 24, near milepost 299, on Manitou Ave.

9 housekeeping cabins/cottages
17 non-housekeeping cabins/cottages
Rates: $$ to $$$$$

Howard Sulzer & Olga Folster
23 Manitou Ave. (CB)
Manitou Springs CO 80829
(719) 685-5485
(800) 782-2246

Pets: No
Elevation: 6,035
Credit Cards: VMAD
Open all year

Green Willow Motel Cottages

Cross a bridge on Fountain Creek to find clean, rustic-style modern cottages at Green Willow Motel. The Heruths provide you with a friendly atmosphere on spacious, tree-lined grounds. All cottages have cable television and showers; some have tubs. The creekside picnic area has picnic tables, grills and a swing set.

Prices vary depending on the time of year. There is a nominal charge for baby beds and cots.

Royal Gorge and Cripple Creek are only an hour's drive away, or you can go on relaxing, sightseeing bus tours. Walk from your cabin to Manitou Springs city parks, Olympic-sized pool, water slide and Garden of the Gods.

Location: Within city limits; on a bus line.

6 housekeeping cottages
8 non-housekeeping cottages
Rates: $$ to $$$

Ron & Bev Heruth
328 Manitou Ave. (CB)
Manitou Springs CO 80829-2506
(719) 685-9997
(719) 685-1645

Pets: No
Elevation: 6,400
Credit Cards: VMD
Open April 15 to October 15

Just-A-Mere Cottage

These fully equipped cottages are set in a quiet area on the lower slopes of Catamount Mountain, in the small resort community of Green Mountain Falls. The cottages are true vacation homes, including daily maid service, fireplaces, washers and dryers, microwave ovens, cable television and telephones.

Reservations and first-night deposit are required. All facilities are easily accessible for older people.

Walk up the stream to the Green Mountain Falls for which the town is named. The town offers restaurants, swimming, fishing, bicycling and hiking trails. All attractions in the Pikes Peak region — Garden of the Gods, the Pikes Peak Cog Railway, Seven Falls, North Pole/Santa's Workshop, the Air Force Academy, Cave of the Winds, Cripple Creek and Victor mining towns, Royal Gorge and beautiful Teller County — are close by so you can enjoy your home away from home in the mountains.

Location: 12 miles west of Colorado Springs on Route 24, in Green Mountain Falls.

2 housekeeping cottages
Rates: $$$$

Tom & Bonnie Acton
10995 Belvidere Ave.
P.O. Box 254 (CB)
Green Mountain Falls CO 80819-0254
(719) 684-9797

Pets: No
Elevation: 8,000
Credit Cards: VM
Open all year

Pinehaven Lodges

These lodges are literally in the shadow of Pikes Peak. The beautiful Ute Pass area stretches out in both directions, furnishing a constantly changing and always restful scene of unmatched beauty. The large cabins, located in Chipita Park and Cascade, are each different; all have fireplaces, living rooms, bedrooms, family rooms, television, fully equipped kitchens and decks or patios with wonderful views.

The lodges' close proximity to Green Mountain Falls and Manitou Springs allows for hiking, jogging, fishing, horseback riding, swimming, bicycling, tennis and dining at nearby restaurants. Pinehaven Lodges is only 20 minutes from Colorado Springs and near to most Pikes Peak area attractions.

Location: 5 and 8 miles west of Manitou Springs on Highway 24. Exit Green Mountain Falls for Chipita Park Road, go left ⅓ mile on a mountain road.

7 housekeeping cabins
Rates: $$$$$

Greg & Cavan-Daly McGrew
Redstone Castle (CB)
Manitou Springs CO 80829
(719) 685-5070
(719) 684-9844
(719) 685-5663

Pets: No
Elevation: 7,000
Credit Cards: No
Open all year

Rainbow Falls Park

Bring your family for a relaxing stay at Colorado's first trout hatchery, established in 1871. There are 25 acres of crystal-clear lakes and streams, all brimming with trout. Cabins overlook the lakes, offering a fantastic view of Pikes Peak. Just bring bedding and cooking utensils to fry your freshly caught trout for breakfast.

Reservations are required for chuckwagon breakfasts and dinners.

Besides excellent fishing with no license required, there are guided horseback rides, hatchery tours, chuckwagon dinners, hayrides, a complete fishing store and playground. Discover a Ute Indian cave, explore a gold mine or backpack into the Rampart Range. Rainbow Falls is close to all Pikes Peak area attractions.

Location: West from Colorado Springs on Highway 24 to Woodland Park, north 10 miles on Highway 67, near milepost 87.

2 housekeeping cabins
Camping available
Rates: $$

Christine & Larry Posik
P.O. Box 9062 (CB)
Woodland Park CO 80866-9062
(719) 687-9074
(719) 687-8676

Pets: Yes
Elevation: 7,500
Credit Cards: VM
Open all year

Red Stone Castle

Built in the 1890s by William Davis, this magnificently restored Victorian luxury bed and breakfast in Manitou Springs is one of Colorado's finest historic residences. Red Stone Castle offers a family invitation into a private 20-acre estate overlooking the National Historic District of Manitou Springs. The Castle, which commands spectacular views of the Garden of the Gods, Iron Mountain, Red Mountain and Colorado Springs, is ideal for an individual, couple or a small family. A most memorable experience!

Located in Manitou Springs, you'll have plenty of opportunity for shopping and fine dining, as well as hiking and sightseeing in the Pikes Peak region.

Location: Take Manitou Avenue to Pawnee Avenue and left on Southside Road to the gate.

1 castle
Rates: $$$$$

Greg and Cavan-Daly McGrew
Redstone Castle (CB)
Manitou Springs CO 80829
(719) 685-5070
(719) 685-5663

Pets: No
Elevation: 7,000
Credit Cards: No
Open all year

Treehaven Cottages

These cottages are available in a variety of sizes, each one with color television, air-conditioning, an outdoor pool and a view of Pikes Peak from the private picnic area. The cottages are in a rustic, tree-shaded setting just below Pikes Peak, but close to attractions and restaurants.

Treehaven's service is helpful and friendly; they'll make reservations for various local attractions and suggest excellent day trips for exploring the Pikes Peak region. Local attractions include the Garden of the Gods, the Pro Rodeo Hall of Fame, the Air Force Academy and the Pikes Peak Cog Railway.

Location: From I-25 take Highway 24 west to Ridge Road, left on Ridge Road to Coloroado Avenue.

12 housekeeping cottages
Rates: Call for prices

Dorothy & Bill Martin
3620 W. Colorado Ave. (CB)
Colorado Springs CO 80904
(719) 578-1968

Pets: No
Elevation: 6,200
Credit Cards: VMD
Open all year

Ute Pass Cabins & Motel

Ute Pass Cabins & Motel is your gateway to Colorado. The motel, originally built in 1895, has been expanded and restored. You'll feel at home in the family sized, kitchen-equipped units. Sleep to the soothing sounds of the ever-gurgling mountain stream that meanders through the grounds. There is a game room and a laundromat and the outdoor picnic area is right on Fountain Creek, so you can eat outdoors amid the scenic splendor.

Experience historic Manitou Springs by taking a walking tour. Visit many of the sights of the Pikes Peak area just a short ride away. Motor up the Ute Pass to the gambling casinos at Cripple Creek. Fish in Fountain Creek on the property or at other nearby mountain streams and lakes. Meals are available one block away at the restored Historical Manitou Spa Building.

Location: In Manitou Springs.

4 housekeeping cabins
13 motel rooms with kitchenette
4 motel rooms without kitchenettes
Rates: Call for prices

Suzie Hawkins
1132 Manitou Ave. (CB)
Manitou Springs CO 80829
Information: (719) 685-5171
Reservations: (800) 845-9762

Pets: No
Elevation: 6,400
Credit Cards: VMA
Open all year

Western Cabins Resort

This resort is a quiet hideaway in Manitou Springs, with The Garden of the Gods as your backyard. All of the rustic, Western-style cabins are equipped with kitchens, private bath and shower, direct dial phones, cable television and air-conditioning. Upper terrace cabins have unobstructed views of Pikes Peak. This resort offers on-site conveniences, such as a laundromat, a beauty and barber shop, a play area, a heated pool, picnic tables, a barbecue area and movies.

You pay lower rates from Labor Day to Memorial Day. Your hosts will arrange sightseeing tours and reservations for chuckwagon dinners, melodramas and the Pikes Peak Cog Railway at no extra charge.

Just three minutes away in downtown Manitou Springs, shop for gifts, antiques and western wear; eat at fine restaurants; try the local mineral water or just browse. Walk a few blocks to restaurants, churches and stables. Manitou Springs is an excellent starting point for many Pikes Peak area attractions.

Location: North of Manitou Ave on Beakers Lane, off Highway 24, near milepost 300.

8 housekeeping cabins
Rates: $$$

Teresa Kerns & Lillian Simek
106 Beckers Lane (CB)
Manitou Springs CO 80829
Information (719) 685-5755
Reservations: (800) 873-4553

Pets: No
Elevation: 6,336
Credit Cards: VMAD
Open all year

Woodland Park Camper Cabins & Campground

Fun, clean and a great place for the family, this campground is high in the mountains amid towering pines. Bring your own bedding and supplies to one of the eight camper cabins. Facilities include a heated pool, free miniature golf, playgrounds, game room, a convenience store with a craft shoppe, laundromat and clean hot showers. You're welcome to start campfires with supplied firewood.

Chow down at the chuckwagon breakfasts and dinners from mid-July to mid-August, then watch free movies on the big screen, shown nightly. Don't forget dessert with the all-you-can-eat ice cream for just $1.00! Conveniently located, the Woodland Park Camper Cabins & Campground is only 16 miles from Colorado Springs attractions. You can also take bus tours of scenic Cripple Creek.

Location: ½ mile north from the intersection of Highways 24 and 67. Look for the sign on the left-hand side of the road through the trees. Turn left and drive three blocks west on Bowman Ave.

8 camper cabins (one with 2 rooms)
Camping available
Rates: $

Craig & Karen Stewart
1125 W. Bowman Ave.
P.O. Box 725 (CB)
Woodland Park CO 80866-0725
(719) 687-3535
Off-season: (719) 599-8486

Pets: Yes
Elevation: 8,500
Credit Cards: VMD
Open May 1 to September 20

Cortez: see Dolores and Mesa Verde Area. Map: O-2

CRAWFORD

Includes Maher. Map: J-6

This is a town where cowboys still wear Stetson hats and spurs, cattle drives take place down Main Street and Western hospitality is a way of life. It is an adventurer's paradise, with outstanding big game hunting, excellent fishing, snowmobiling, cross-country and downhill skiing, ice skating, four-wheel drive tours and hiking. In addition, the spectacular Black Canyon of the Gunnison and Needle Rock provide photographers with spectacular views.

Fun Things to Do

- Crawford State Park (303) 921-5721
- North Rim of the Black Canyon of the Gunnison National Monument (303)249-7036

Becker Ranch Bed & Breakfast

Becker Ranch is a spacious stone country home located on 40 acres in one of Colorado's most picturesque valleys. The Becker's home becomes yours during your family getaway and they serve breakfasts made with local homemade sausages, too! Amenities include satellite television, a swimming pool, a children's playground and lots of room to roam.

Children are always welcome.

Nearby, go hunting, fishing, hiking, river rafting, water-skiing, snowmobiling and downhill and cross-country skiing. Becker Ranch is near the spectacular north rim of the Black Canyon of the Gunnison. Enjoy several local, summertime festivals, such as the Delta County Fair and the Little Britches Rodeo.

Location: Approximately 8 miles south of Hotchkiss on Highway 92, near milepost 29.

4 bed and breakfast rooms
Rates: $$$

Myron E. & Joan Becker
3798 Highway 92 (CB)
Crawford CO 81415
(303) 921-6877
(800) 392-3765

Pets: No
Elevation: 6,800
Credit Cards: No
Open all year

Campstool Ranch

Enjoy the beautiful scenery of Black Mesa in this unique rock house built in 1912. The house is on the old Ute Trail, over which cattle were brought into the valley by the first settlers. The Campstool's hospitality includes your choice of the continental-style breakfast or the "rancher" breakfast.

Campstool Ranch is near the north rim of the Black Canyon of the Gunnison, Crawford Reservoir, Grand Mesa and the Blue Mesa Reservoir. This is excellent country for big-game hunting and lake and stream fishing. In the summer, go water-skiing, boating, river rafting, hiking, or golfing. In the winter, go cross-country and downhill skiing, snowmobiling, ice fishing and skating.

Location: On the West Elk Loop Scenic Byway, Highway 92, near milepost 37.

3 bed and breakfast rooms
Rates: $$ to $$$

George & Winnie Tracy
80367 Highway 92
P.O. Box 14 (CB)
Maher CO 81421
(303) 921-6461

Pets: Yes
Elevation: 7,000
Credit Cards: No
Open June 1 to November 30

Last Frontier Lodge

Take a vacation to the lodge on the lake, away from shopping malls, highways and condos. This modern lodge is in a part of Colorado where the Old West is still a natural and daily way of life.

When you make reservations, specify whether you want bed and breakfast or all meals

Relax, enjoy good food and explore the best of Colorado's lakes, rivers and wilderness. Rent horses or hike into the West Elk Wilderness, with its undisturbed lakes, sparkling streams, mountain peaks and canyons. Your hosts work with local cattle ranchers and outfitters for special vacation activities. Ask about the special cattle drives and spring horse roundup.

Location: Off Highway 92, near milepost 32.

6 housekeeping cabins
9 lodge rooms
Rates: Call for prices

Clair & Nola Hicks
4020 C Highway 92;
P.O. Box 162 (CB)
Crawford CO 81415-0162
(303) 921-6363

Pets: Yes
Elevation: 7,000
Credit Cards: VM
Open all year

CREEDE

Also see South Fork. Map: M9

Located high in the Rockies at 8,854 feet, near the headwaters of the Rio Grande, the beauty of the area is breathtaking. In its heyday, Creede was unsurpassed as a mining town — it was one of the richest and wildest camps in the 1890s. Today, the old mining town atmosphere still exists in restaurants, shops and the Creede Repertory Theater. In the summer, miles of marked roads and trails, rivers, streams and numerous lakes offer unlimited opportunities to the outdoor enthusiast. The turning of the Aspen leaves adds spectacular color. Cross-country skiing, snowmobiling, ice fishing, sledding and tubing make this area into a winter wonderland. Whatever you are looking for in natural beauty, you'll find it in Creede.

Fun Things to Do

- Broadacres Stables (719) 658-2291
- Creede Museum (800) 327-2102
- Creede Underground Firehouse (719) 658-2600
- The Wood Gallery (719) 658-2423
- Underground Mining Museum (719)658-0406

Antlers Ranch

Homesteaded in 1896, Antlers Ranch is a picturesque mountain retreat nestled between the banks of the sparkling Rio Grande and the Silver Thread Scenic Byway. Most of the secluded modern cabins and rooms have gas heat, two double or queen-sized beds, bathroom with a shower, a porch with a swing, bed linens and fully equipped kitchenettes. Ranch facilities include a recreation room, a children's playground and a laundromat.

Antlers Ranch offers daily, weekly and group rates.

A fish fry/potluck is a weekly highlight at the ranch, where you can also get fishing licenses and supplies. The 70 acres of Antlers Ranch are surrounded by the Rio Grande National Forest, which provides unlimited activities for spring, summer and fall enjoyment. Popular sports include fishing, hiking, river rafting on the Rio Grande, mountain bike tours and horseback riding.

Location: 5 miles southwest of Creede, just off Highway 149, near milepost 26.

13 housekeeping cabins
9 motel rooms with kitchenette
Rates: cabins $$$$, rooms $$$

Stanley & Zelda Meer McCrossen
HC 70 (CB)
Creede CO 81130
October through April:
369 West 23rd Street
Durango CO 81301
(719) 658-2423
Winter: (303) 247-3923

Pets: Yes (declare at registration)
Elevation: 9,000
Credit Cards: VM
Open May 1 to October 15

Broadacres Guest Ranch

Broadacres Ranch is connected with a working cattle ranch. A "heavenly place" to relax, play and enjoy a ranch atmosphere with picture-perfect scenery, these are fully furnished two- and three-bedroom modern cottages, some overlooking the river.

Fish in the river, in nearby streams and at a private lake. Take horseback rides along scenic mountain trails — the ranch borders National Forest lands.

Location: 4 miles southwest of Creede just off Highway 149, near milepost 25.

12 housekeeping cottages
Camping available
Rates: $$ to $$$$$

Bea Collerette
P.O. Box 39 (CB)
Creede CO 81130
(719) 658-2291

Pets: Yes
Elevation: 8,887
Credit Cards: No
Open May 15 to October 30

Soward Ranch

Off the beaten path in a scenic valley on the Rio Grande, Soward Ranch is a resort and cattle ranch that has been in the same family for over 100 years. Surrounded by mountains, the large property has six lakes with outstanding views. Each cabin, located apart from the others to ensure privacy, are fully modernized with full bath, gas heating for cooking and electricity. If you want to rough it, you can in one of the ranch's two pioneer cabins. Dishes, silver, utensils, bedding and linen are furnished in all cabins.

Advance reservations are required.

Fish for trout on the property along several miles of creeks, on the Rio Grande and at three small private lakes. Soward Ranch is also close to many other state-stocked lakes, reservoirs and streams.

Location: 14 miles southwest of Creede, off of Highway 149, near milepost 28.

12 housekeeping cabins
Rates: $$ to $$$$

Howard, Margaret, Scott & Steve Lamb
P.O. Box 130 (CB)
Creede CO 81130-0130
(719) 658-2295
Winter: (719) 658-2228

Pets: No
Elevation: 9,000
Credit Cards: No
Open May 26 to October 7

CRESTED BUTTE

Also see Gunnison. Map: I-9

Crested Butte, surrounded by sheer beauty, is the place to raft down a whitewater river or relax in a hot tub. Home of the Fat Tire Bike Week, the oldest bike festival in the world, you can mountain bike down a scenic pass or Jeep to an old ghost town. Try fly-fishing in nearby streams or play a championship golf course, savor campfire cuisine or gourmet restaurants, catch a play or climb a peak — there's something for everyone. As the wildflower capital of Colorado, Crested Butte basks in gentle mountain warmth, an inspiration for recreationists and nature lovers. During the winter, Crested Butte, Mt. Crested Butte and Crested Butte Ski Area are connected by a free shuttle. With an average of 229 inches of snow each year, this is a great area for winter sports, including snowmobiling, downhill and cross-country skiing.

Fun Things to Do

- Mountain Bike Hall of Fame Museum (303) 349-7382
- Skyland Resort & Country Club (303) 394-6131
- Three Rivers Outfitting, Rafting & Willow Fly Anglers (303) 641-1303

Star Valley Ranch

Only 7 miles from historic Crested Butte, Star Valley Ranch is located in the Gunnison National Forest. The cabins, built in the 1930s, are set well away from each other to provide a feeling of privacy not often found in other cabin resorts. Each one features fully equipped kitchens, wood-burning stoves or fireplaces and bathrooms with showers. All of the double beds are fitted with linens and cozy down comforters.

Off-season discounts are offered in the fall and spring months.

In the summer, hiking trails and challenging single-track mountain bike routes begin from your front door. Fishing from Cement Creek is only 50 yards away. In the winter, ski downhill slopes at nearby Mt. Crested Butte, or cross-country ski in the back-country of the National Forest. During the fall and spring months, the area is less crowded, but no less beautiful, with spring wildflowers and autumn colors.

Location: Take Highway 135 north from Gunnison. Turn east (right) at milepost 20 on Cement Creek Road. Continue 2 miles.

8 housekeeping cabins/cottages
Rates: $$$$ to $$$$$

Mike & Sara Martin
Cement Creek Rd. (CB)
Crested Butte CO 81224
(303) 349-5517

Pets: No
Elevation: 8,900
Credit Cards: VM
Open all year

CRIPPLE CREEK

Includes Victor. Map: I-16

Step back a century when you visit this historic mining town. Discover the old mining camps from your vehicle as you drive through the area, or walk through historic Bennett Avenue to experience the booming, gold rush days when gold fever ran rampant. The casinos echo the glory days of hustle and bustle as you tempt "lady luck." Outdoor enthusiasts can find abundant fishing and hiking in the adjoining three million acres of Pike National Forest. This pocket of history, some 10,000 feet above sea level and just west of Pikes Peak, sits in the center of some of the most magnificent scenery Colorado has to offer.

Fun Things to Do

- Cripple Creek & Victor Narrow Gauge Railroad (719) 689-2640
- Cripple Creek District Museum (719) 689-2634
- Cripple Creek Golf Course (719) 689-2531
- The Old Homestead Parlour House Museum (719) 689-3090
- Victor/Lowell Thomas Museum, Victor (719) 689-2766

Cripple Creek Gold Camper Cabins & Campground

Conveniently located just around the bend from the Old West town of Cripple Creek and next to the Pike National Forest, these camper cabins are a great way to visit this gold-mining area. Bring your own bedding and cooking supplies — they furnish the firewood. Facilities include hot showers, a laundromat, playground and game room.

Hike or ride horseback in nearby Pike National Forest. You can see elk, deer, mountain sheep and antelope from time to time just short distances from the campground. Parking your RV is easy when you shop in Cripple Creek, visit museums of the old west and gamble in the area's many casinos.

Location: 5 miles north of Cripple Creek on Highway 67, near milepost 58,12 miles south of the Continental Divide.

2 camper cabins
Camping available
Rates: $

William & Linda Buckhanan
12654 Highway 67 North
P.O. Box 601 (CB)
Cripple Creek CO 80813
(719) 689-2342

Pets: Yes
Elevation: 10,200
Credit Cards: No
Open all year

Cripple Creek Travel Park & Hospitality House

This is a truly unique accommodation — the 18 guest rooms were created in a restored Victorian county hospital. These rooms range from small, old-fashioned singles with an antique corner washbowl to large, family units with full private baths. Other facilities include a bathhouse, a laundromat, children's playground, picnic tables, grills and a covered picnic area. A family recreation room provides cable television and HBO.

Cripple Creek Travel Park & Hospitality House is within city limits of Cripple Creek, close to all attractions.

Location: Go west on Bennett Avenue to B Street, then north 6 blocks.

18 lodge rooms
5 on-site trailers
Camping available
Rates: $$$ to $$$$

Steve & Bonnie Mackin
600 North B St.
P.O. Box 957 (CB)
Cripple Creek CO 80813
(719) 689-2513

Pets: No
Elevation: 9,494
Credit Cards: VMD
Open May 25 to September 30

Pikes Peak Outfitters and Cabins

Pikes Peak Outfitters is a year-round operation, with special summer activities provided from April through August. You can stay in full service rooms, which includes all meals, or you can rent cabins as a bed and breakfast.

In the summer, they offer horseback rides and free horseback riding lessons; steak dinner and moonlight rides; and fishing, wilderness survival and photography trips. These trips include guides, food, lodging, hot showers and campfires at night, with outings to the casinos in Cripple Creek during the day. In the winter, you can enjoy ice fishing, winter hunting and cross-country skiing.

Location: On Gold Camp Road, 15 minutes outside of Victor, near Cripple Creek.

5 housekeeping cabins
Rates: $$$ to $$$$$

Jim & Sharon Nothstein
120 W Woodland Ave.
P.O. Box 9053(CB)
Woodland Park CO 80866-9053
(719) 687-0482
(800) 748-2885

Pets: No
Elevation: 10,200
Credit Cards: No
Open all year

DELTA

Also see Grand Mesa Area and Paonia. Map: J-4

Delta is fun in all seasons. You can experience the past hidden in the canyons west of town, where two of the largest dinosaur bones ever found were recently discovered. The area is rich in Ute Indian lore — the Ute Council Tree, 1 mile north of town, was an important gathering spot. Once homesteaders arrived in Delta, they shared the wild west with notorious outlaws such as Butch Cassidy and the McCarty brothers. The mild climate and fertile soil make this an outstanding fruit-producing area; many tourists arrive in late summer to pick peaches, apples, sweet-and-sour cherries, pears, apricots and plums. The area also offers a multitude of activities for the outdoor enthusiasts: tennis, golfing, fishing, hiking and hunting.

Fun Things to Do

- Cottonwood Golf Course (303) 874-7263
- Delta Historical Society (303) 874-9721
- Fort Uncompahgre (303) 874-7566
- Thunder Mountain Productions (303) 874-8616 or (303) 874-8305

25 Mesa Ranch

Relax with home-style hospitality in the scenic Southwest mountains. On the Uncompahgre Plateau, surrounded by the Uncompahgre National Forest, two secluded cabins are nestled in ponderosa pines. Stay for an hour, a day, a week or a month. Besides outdoor sports, you can curl up with a book under a tall pine tree or relax in the wood-fired hot tub after a full day of activity.

Reservations are required.

Mesa Ranch rents horses for riding, or they can arrange backpacking and four-wheel drive trips. Be sure to ask about the excellent elk and deer hunting locations.

Location: 22 miles southwest of Delta.

1 housekeeping cabin
1 non-housekeeping cabin
Rates: $$ to $$$$$

Max & Judy Ungerer
P.O. Box 787 (CB)
Delta CO 81416-0787
(800) 533-8446

Pets: Yes
Elevation: 7,500
Credit Cards: No
Open April 1 through December 1

DENVER AREA

Includes Aurora, Broomfield, Golden and Strasburg. Also see Bailey, El Rancho and Evergreen. Map: F-17

Denver is known as "The Queen City of the Plains" and as "The Mile High City." Located just east of the Rocky Mountains, Denver has a mild climate with only 15 inches of precipitation a year — and more annual hours of sunshine than Miami or San Diego. The city has a variety of attractions to meet every taste and budget, including free walking tours, the U.S. Mint, the Denver Art Museum (which has the world's greatest collection of Indian art) and the Colorado State Capital Building Rotunda, where you can stand 1 mile above sea level and have the best view of over 150 miles of snow-covered peaks. Denver has parks and gardens, museums, shopping, night life, restaurants from casual to elegant, theater and sporting events. There's something for everyone in Colorado's capital.

Fun Things to Do

- Black American West Museum & Heritage Center (303) 292-2566
- Buffalo Bill Memorial Museum, Golden (303) 526-0744
- Children's Museum (303) 866-3682
- Colorado School of Mines & Geology Museum, Golden (303) 273-3823
- Denver Art Museum (303) 575-2793
- Denver Botanical Gardens (303) 331-4000
- Denver City Park Golf Course (303) 295-2095
- Denver Museum of Natural History (303) 322-7009
- Denver Zoological Gardens (303) 331-4100
- Echo Lake Lodge Restaurant (303) 567-2138
- El Rancho Restaurant ((303) 526-0661, Fax: (303) 526-0674
- Harvard Gulch Golf Course (303) 698-4078
- Molly Brown House (303) 832-4092
- Mountain View Golf Course (303) 694-3012
- Overland Park Golf Course (303) 777-7331
- Park Hill Golf Course (303) 333-5411
- Rio Grande Ski Train, Denver to Winter Park (303) 296-4754
- United States Mint (303) 844-3332
- Wellshire Golf Course (303) 757-1352
- Willis Case Golf Course (303) 455-9801

Denver East/Strasburg KOA & Kamping Kabins™

These camping cabins offer a pleasant and inexpensive place to stay while seeing the sights of the Denver area. The tree-filled campground provides you with all conveniences — hot showers, laundromat, store, playground, game room, a swimming pool and a pleasant surrounding.

Groups are encouraged and welcome.

All of the attractions of Denver are within an easy drive, including the zoo and the Museum of Natural History. See the local Comanche Crossing Museum in Strasburg, with a restored train depot and other early buildings and exhibits.

Location: Highway 70, Exit 310, 35 miles east of Denver.

6 camper cabins
Camping available
Rates: $

Jim & Sharon Strange
1312 Monroe St.
P.O. Box 597 (CB)
Strasburg CO 80136-0597
(303) 622-9274

Pets: Yes
Elevation: 5,380
Credit Cards: VMD
Open all year

Denver Meadows Camper Cabins & RV Park

Located on the edge of Denver, this park sports a swimming pool, a hot tub, private showers, laundromat facilities, a game room and many other amenities.

Denver Meadows is centrally located for seeing Denver and the Rockies and is near to the city buses and shopping centers. If you're interested in sightseeing tours, just ask your hosts to arrange them.

Location: Exit I-225 at East Colfax, near milepost 10. Go 200 yards west, then 3 blocks north on Potomac.

3 camper cabins
Camping available
Rates: $

Shawn Lustigman, Owner
Teddy Cline & Ralph Shaoul, Managers
2075 Potomac St. (CB)
Aurora CO 80011
(303) 364-9483
Fax: (303) 366-7289

Pets: Yes (small indoor pets only)
Elevation: 5,280
Credit Cards: VM
Open all year

Denver North Camper Cabins & Campground

In a quiet countryside location, yet centrally located for Denver area attractions, camper cabins are an inexpensive way to stay when visiting the area. This campground has a swimming pool, barbecue grills, clean showers and a grocery store. They serve pancake breakfasts six days a week during the summer.

A good location close to the sights of Denver, Boulder and Rocky Mountain National Park.

Location: I-25, exit 229 (15 miles north of I-70).

2 camper cabins
Camping available
Rates: $

Jerry & Sue Maloney
16700 N. Washington (CB)
Broomfield CO 80020
(303) 452-4120

Pets: Yes
Elevation: 5,280
Credit Cards: VM
Open all year

Dillon: see Summit County. Map: F-13

Dinosaur National Monument: see Meeker. Map: E-5

DIVIDE

Map: I-16

In the heart of Pikes Peak country, there is something special: beautiful scenery, wildlife, intricate fossils, silvery trout, winding trails, interesting history and countless places of solitude. Florissant Fossil Beds National Monument, only a short distance away, appears to be an empty valley, but after stopping at the visitor center to learn how to spot fossils, you'll find fossilized insects, plant life and enormous trees dating back some 35 million years. The monument grounds also contain the 160-acre Hornbeck Homestead, demonstrating the harsh life of homesteaders 100 years ago. At the nearby 7,000-acre Dome Rock State Wildlife Area, you'll see Rocky Mountain bighorn sheep, deer, elk, bobcats, coyotes, eagles and wild turkeys basking in the shadow of Pikes Peak.

Fun Things to Do

- Florissant Fossil Beds National Monument (303) 748-3253

Colorado Mountain Ranch

This modern log cabin provides quiet relaxation and a rustic atmosphere. Settle in and make yourself at home with a fireplace, full kitchen and a large bathroom, in a cabin surrounded by trees and mountain views.

Reservation and deposit are required. Be sure to reserve a space for your horse in their well-equipped horse boarding facility.

Colorado Mountain Ranch is only 45 minutes from Pikes Peak attractions, whitewater rafting, horseback riding, hiking and world-class fishing. Do as much or as little as you desire here.

Location: Located 1 mile north of Highway 24.

1 housekeeping cabin
Rates: $$$

Charles & Susan Pierce
290 Aspen Dr.
P.O. Box 366 (CB)
Divide CO 80814-0366
(719) 687-6718

Pets: Yes
Elevation: 9,200
Credit Cards: None
Open all year

DOLORES

Includes Stoner and Rico. Map: O-3

Dolores has it all, from mountain scenery to the second largest lake in Colorado, McPhee Lake, where you can enjoy boating, fishing and water-skiing. More than 1 million fish, including bass, crappie and catfish are stocked in the lake for the finest fishing in the Southwest. The high country waters of the Dolores River Valley are teaming with Rainbow, Brown, Cutthroat and Brook trout. This area also has excellent hunting, with an abundance of wildlife and big game. You can see the area's beautiful archeology depicted in the nearby Anasazi Heritage Center and Escalante Ruins. Enjoy outdoor recreation at its finest: hike, jeep, or horseback ride in the San Juan National Forest, from the Dolores River Valley to 14,000-foot peaks in the Mount Wilson Primitive Area.

Fun Things to Do

- Anasazi Heritage Center (303) 882-4811
- Conquistador Golf Course (303) 565-9208
- Crow Canyon Archeological Center (800) 422-8975
- Dolores River Line Camp Chuckwagon Supper & Western Show (303) 882-4158
- Mesa Verde Cortez Information Center (800) 346-6528
- Stoner Lodge Restaurant (303) 882-7825

Circle "K" Guest Ranch

Nestled in the San Juan National Forest on the Dolores River, Circle "K" has a lodge, bunkhouses, housekeeping cabins, motel units, and RV and tentsites. They also provide full meals throughout your stay.

Circle "K" specializes in family reunions and church retreats; they have group rates — the full-service plan provides big savings.

The ranch offers day camp activities, including horseback riding lessons, rail rides, fishing, river tug-of-war, calf catching, river swimming, an obstacle course and a mountain cable slide. Join them for the Rocky Mountain Gospel Music Festival in the summer! There are also many four-wheel drive roads and mining camps nearby.

Location: Highway 145, near milepost 36, 26 miles northeast of Dolores.

3 housekeeping cabins
8 motel rooms without kitchenette
Large bunkhouses
Camping available
Rates: $ to $$$$

Al, Joan, John, & Wanda Cannon
26916 Highway 145 (CB)
Dolores CO 81323
(303) 562-3808

Pets: No
Elevation: 8,000
Credit Cards: None
Open all year

Green Snow Oasis

Come visit during the hunting season! About 6 miles south of Rico on the Dolores River, you'll find cabins that sleep six, with full baths, kitchen and wood-burning stoves. A gift shop has homemade quilts, local crafts, Indian jewelry and antiques.

The Green Snow Oasis is near to Telluride, Cortez, Mancos and Durango. Enjoy the excellent trout fishing and hunting.

Location: Highway 145, near milepost 40.

4 housekeeping cabins/cottages
Rates: $$$

Ouida North
27602 Highway 145 (CB)
Dolores CO 81323
(303) 562-3829

Pets: Yes (extra fee)
Elevation: 8,300
Credit Cards: None
Open April 15 to November 15

Groundhog Lake Cabins, Campground & Outfitters

In the heart of the San Juan Mountains, you'll find excellent fishing, camping and hunting off the beaten path. You can rent boats and buy bait, fishing licenses and food at the convenience store.

Enjoy the weekly fish fries, where you'll hear great fish stories. Your hosts also offer outfitter guide service during elk and deer season. Or, with advance registration, you can try a one- to three-day mountain horse pack trip.

Location: In Dolores, turn on 11th Street at the General store; go 28 miles north on gravel Dolores/Norwood Road. Then turn right on Route 533, 4 miles to the lake.

1 housekeeping cabin
1 non-housekeeping cabin
1 on-site trailer for rent
Camping available
Rates: $

Jim & Louanne Wagoner
15525 County Road32
P.O. Box 27 (CB)
Dolores CO 81323-0027
June–October using a touch tone-phone:
(303) 565-8974 when you hear another
tone push 20184.
all year: (303) 882-4379

Pets: Yes
Elevation: 9,000
Credit Cards: None
Open May 25 to November 1

Lost Canyon Lake Lodge

In a contemporary log home nestled in tall pines overlooking Lost Canyon Lake Reservoir, you'll find four comfortable bedrooms with private baths. Relax by the fireplace in the lounge and enjoy an evening coffee or glass of sherry. The room rate includes large, continental breakfasts with homemade muffins, seasonal fruits, fresh-ground coffee and various hot dishes that you may eat indoors or on the wrap-around deck. You can also order full breakfasts.

Reservations are recommended. Children are welcome in this non-smoking lodge.

Lost Canyon is only 20 minutes from Mesa Verde National Park. Your hosts are happy to give sightseeing tips and help arrange memorable adventures, from canoeing and horseback riding to archaeological digs and hot-air ballooning.

Location: Between Dolores and Mancos, north of Highway 184, near milepost 16.

4 lodge rooms
Rates: Call for prices

Beth Newman & Ken Nickson
P.O. Box 1289 (CB)
Dolores CO 81323-1289
☏800) 992-1098
(303) 882-4913

Pets: No
Elevation: 7,300
Credit Cards: VM
Open all year

Outpost Cabins, RV Park & Motel

Enjoy cool mountain air, fish from the deck, or just relax on the beautiful Dolores River. These cabins come equipped with everything except cooking utensils — housekeepers even clean daily. There is an on-site laundromat for your convenience.

Have a barbecue under the trees by the river, or go to nearby McPhee Reservoir for the best bass and trout fishing in Colorado. Don't forget to visit the Anasazi Heritage Center, Mesa Verde National Park and the Escalante Ruins, all just a short distance away.

Location: In Dolores, 10 miles north of Cortez on Highway 145.

3 housekeeping cabins
7 motel rooms with kitchenettes
3 motel rooms without kitchenettes
camping available
Rates: $$ to $$$$

Ray & Darlene LeBlanc
1800 Highway 145
P.O. Box 295 (CB)
Dolores CO 81323-0295
(303) 882-7271
(800) 382-4892

Pets: Yes
Elevation: 6,900
Credit Cards: VMAD
Open all year

Priest Gulch Cabins, Campground & RV Park

Stay in an idyllic setting in a beautiful river valley. Some of these deluxe cabins have decks over the Dolores River — one is on a creek that runs through the property. All have kitchens, dining rooms, bathrooms, linens, dishes, television and fishing opportunities. Larger cabins also have living rooms. A grocery store, playground and laundromat are conveniently located on the premises. If you feel chilly or have a hankering to roast marshmallows, ask for free firewood.

Local activities include trout fishing, elk hunting, hiking and backpacking in the 14,000-foot peaks of the San Juan National Forest. Explore four-wheel drive roads or pan for gold — the hosts will even lend you a gold pan to try your luck!

Location: 35 miles northeast of Cortez on Highway 145, near milepost 35½.

1 camper cabin
4 housekeeping cabins
1 on-site trailer
Camping available
Rates: Call for prices

Ernie & Margaret Allsup
26750 Highway 145 (CB)
Dolores CO 81323
(303) 562-3810

Pets: Yes
Elevation: 8,100
Credit Cards: VM
Open May 1 to November 15

Rag O'Muffin Ranch

Rag O'Muffin Ranch sits beside the Dolores River in a secluded 12-acre location on the San Juan Skyway, with spectacular scenery all year. The two new deluxe housekeeping cottages at Rag O'Muffin Ranch are each furnished with a dishwasher, microwave oven, refrigerator, living and dining area, master bedroom with a queen-sized bed and a loft with twin beds. You bring the food and charcoal; they provide the linens, towels and soap.

They require a two-night minimum stay, but you can rent by the week or month, too.

The property abuts the San Juan National Forest, convenient for hiking, fishing and jeep touring. The ranch is only 22 miles from McPhee Reservoir, the best trout and bass fishing around; 40 miles from Mesa Verde National Park with its ancient cliff dwellings; and 40 miles from Telluride, with skiing in the winter and music festivals in the summer.

Location: Highway 145, near milepost 31½.

2 housekeeping cottages
Rates: $$$$$

Oliver & Joan Chapman
26030 Highway 145 (CB)
Dolores CO 81323
(303) 562-3803

Pets: Yes
Elevation: 7,800
Credit Cards: VM
Open all year

Stoner Cabins & RV Park

Relax and enjoy the mountain grandeur on this quiet, 5½-acre site, lush with tall pines in the heart of the Dolores River Valley. Stoner Cabins has fully furnished units and mobile homes conveniently located next to a store, cafe, gift shop, showers, laundromat and public phones.

Fish the Dolores River, McPhee Lake and miles of nearby mountain streams, or hunt deer and elk in the wooded areas. You can also hike in the nearby San Juan National Forest.

Location: 25½ miles northeast of Cortez, on Highway 145, near milepost 25.

3 housekeeping cottages
1 non-housekeeping cottage
3 on-site trailers
Camping available
Rates: $$ to $$$

Fred & Elnora Muller
25113 Highway 145 (CB)
Dolores CO 81323
(303) 882-4334

Pets: Yes
Elevation: 7,500
Credit Cards: VM
Open May 1 to November 12

Stoner Lodge

This family owned and operated lodge, secluded on the Dolores River, is a high-country treasure, with comfortable rooms and home-cooked meals. You'll enjoy relaxing in the friendly lounge or game room after your day on the Scenic Skyway. If you prefer, you can rent bed and breakfast rooms.

Take your pick of nearby activities, from touring the Indian ruins at Mesa Verde, boating on McPhee Reservoir, fishing for trout in the mountain streams or riding the Durango-Silverton Narrow Gauge Railroad.

Location: 12 miles north of Dolores just off of Highway 145, near milepost 25.

10 lodge rooms
Rates: $$ to $$$

Boss & Tammy Wright
25134 Highway 145 (CB)
Dolores CO 81323
(303) 882-7825

Pets: Yes
Elevation: 7,460
Credit Cards: VM
Open all year

DURANGO

Also see Mesa Verde Area and Vallecito Lake Area. Map: P-5

Durango, surrounded by the San Juan Mountains, lies in the heart of the Four Corners Region. This historic towns is bustling with activity. The famous Durango-Silverton Narrow Gauge Railroad offers the experience of the country's only coal- and steam-powered train that operates daily — you're in true railroading paradise where Mother Nature and the Iron Horse combine their talents to provide an unforgettable experience. There are plenty of other fun activities to keep you busy: rafting, golfing, mountain biking, fishing, horseback riding, skiing, western theater, ballooning, shopping at factory outlets, fine dining, art galleries, rodeos, Indian arts, boating, hiking and much more. Each of Durango's seasons holds its own special magic.

Fun Things to Do

- Animas School Museum (303) 259-2402
- Bar D Chuckwagon Suppers (303) 247-5753
- Durango-Silverton Narrow Gauge Railroad (303) 247-2733
- Hillcrest Golf Course (303) 247-1499
- Mountain Waters Rafting (303) 259-4191 or (800) 748-2507
- Tamarron Golf Course (303) 259-2000
- Trimble Hot Springs (303) 247-0111
- Wildcat Canyon Horse Rides (303) 247-3350 or (800) 748-1711

Durango East KOA & Kamping Kabins™

The closest KOA to Durango, these camper cabins offer a beautiful view of the mesa area. Bring your own cooking gear and bedding, and be ready for swimming in the heated pool, eating delicious pancake breakfasts and barbecue dinners, watching free nightly movies and enjoying ice cream socials throughout the summer. All year, take advantage of the miniature golf course and game room.

Camper cabins book early, so make reservations as soon as you know your travel dates.

Nearby, you'll find a myriad of activities, including raft trips and horseback riding. Your hosts can book reservations for the Durango-Silverton Narrow Gauge Railroad. And Mesa Verde is only 43 miles away.

Location: 5 miles east of Durango city limits on the south side of Highway 160, near milepost 91.

9 camper cabins
Camping available
Rates: $$

Jay & Carol Coates
30090 Highway 160 (CB)
Durango CO 81301-8289
(303) 247-0783

Pets: Yes
Elevation: 7,000
Credit Cards: VMD
Open May 1 to October 15

Durango North (Ponderosa)KOA & Kamping Kabins™

Enjoy a vacation paradise next to the Animas River in the majestic mountains, amid lush oak and towering pines. Bring your own cooking gear and bedding for these comfortable camper cabins. On-site facilities include a large recreation hall and a heated pool. The cafe serves large breakfasts and dinners; after dinner, take in a free movie right on the premises.

Local activities include four-wheel driving, trail biking and hiking and horseback riding. You can fish from the property, either in the Animas River or in their stocked fish pond. In the Durango area, you'll find an alpine slide, the Durango-Silverton Narrow Gauge Railroad and Mesa Verde National Park.

Location: 10 miles north of Durango on Highway 550. Exit County Road 250, near milepost 35½.

12 camper cabins
Camping available
Rates: $ to $$

John & Adeline Harvey
13391 County Road 250 (CB)
Durango CO 81301-8687
(303) 247-4499

Pets: Yes
Elevation: 7,000
Credit Cards: VMDA
Open May 1 to October 16

Lightner Creek Camper Cabins & Campground

Lightner Creek is a 30-acre family resort beside a clear mountain stream. These camper cabins have two double beds stacked as bunks. Cabins have lighting (but no electricity), a picnic table and a fire ring with free firewood. Bring sleeping bags, cooking equipment and pillows. Lightner Creek features a heated pool, a playground, dust-free paved roads, clean restrooms with hot showers, a recreation room, grocery store and laundromat.

Situated only minutes from the Durango-Silverton Narrow Gauge Railroad and downtown Durango, this is an excellent location for exploring the many Durango attractions. Visit the Aztec Ruins National Monument, the Animas River, the San Juan Skyway and many hiking/biking trails.

Location: 2½ miles west of Durango, off of Highway 160, near milepost 80, then 1½ miles north on Lightner Creek Road.

6 camper cabins
Camping available
Rates: $

Joe & Cheryl Amorelli
1567 County Rd. 207 (CB)
Durango CO 81301
(303) 247-5406

Pets: Yes
Elevation: 7,200
Credit Cards: VM
Open May 1 to September 30

Logwood Lodge Bed & Breakfast, The Verheyden Inn

The owners' motto, "Come home to Logwood," says it all. This luxurious, Western red cedar structure is a well-designed bed and breakfast lodge. You can view the beauty of the upper Animas River valley through your room's large windows. Every room features its own private bath and special amenities. Lounge on the deck or in the hammock, or fish in the river while enjoying the beautiful views and river sounds. Wake up to full country breakfasts, while in the evenings, enjoy the cozy fire and savor their award-winning desserts!

Older children are welcome in these non-smoking accommodations.

Only 15 minutes from downtown Durango and the Purgatory ski area and an hour from Mesa Verde National Park. Enjoy fishing and hiking in nearby lakes and trails. Your hosts are happy to supply tour and activity information to make your stay exciting and enjoyable.

Location: North of Durango, off of Highway 550, near milepost 35.

6 bed and breakfast lodge rooms
Rates: $$$$$

Greg & Debby Verheyden
35060 Highway 550 N (CB)
Durango CO 81301
(303) 259-4396
(800) 369-4082

Pets: No
Elevation: 6,750
Credit Cards: VM
Open all year

O-Bar-O Resort

Disappear for awhile in a secluded setting among numerous pine trees and lush grounds. These nicely decorated, riverfront housekeeping cabins have stone fireplaces, fully equipped kitchens, and linens and towels. Each has been remodeled and decorated to offer comfort, but retains a touch of the past.

Reservations are required.

Be sure to cast your fishing rod on the Florida (pronounced *Flor-EED-ah*) River, right outside your door. The resort is only 12 miles from Durango, with its melodrama dinner theater and Durango-Silverton Narrow Gauge Railroad. Other close-in activities include lake and stream fishing, boating, hiking, horseback riding and fine dining.

Location: 12 miles northeast of Durango, about halfway to Vallecito Lake on the Florida River.

6 housekeeping cabins
Rates: $$$$ to $$$$$

Dusty & Claire Walker
11998 County Rd. 240 (CB)
Durango CO 81301-8489
(303) 259-3649

Pets: Yes
Elevation: 7,800
Credit Cards: VM
Open May 15 to October 15

EL RANCHO

Also see Denver Area and Evergreen. Map: F-15

El Rancho is just west of Denver, near the high peaks — a perfect place to stay while visiting both Denver and the ski towns along Interstate 70. It's close to the city in a gorgeous mountain setting. There are abundant historical sites, such as Lookout Mountain and Buffalo Bill's Grave, to explore nearby.

El Rancho Mountain Lodge and Restaurant

Eight individually decorated guest rooms capture a bit of Colorado's colors, history and ambiance: El Rancho has a Southwest feel with tile floor, stucco walls and decorative wall tiles; East Garden I and II feature a floral theme borrowed from the flower gardens on the east patio; the Outpost room is woodsy and masculine with a hunting theme; the Bunkhouse showcases cowboy memorabilia; Alpine I and II have wonderful mountain views and skiing artifacts; and the Cabin's warm, romantic feel comes from a beamed ceiling, stucco walls, luxurious bath and colorful throw rugs. The restaurant serves breakfast, lunch and dinner daily. There's also a Southwestern gift shop, U.S. Post Office and banquet facilities.

El Rancho is conveniently located 18 miles from Denver on I-70. The area offers skiing and hiking close by.

Location: Take exit 252 from I-70.

8 lodge rooms
Rates: Call for prices

R.D. "Skip" & Mary Roush
El Rancho Postal Station (CB)
El Rancho CO 80401
(303) 526-0661
Fax: (303) 526-0674

Pets: No
Elevation: 7,686
Credit Cards: VMAD
Open all year

Eldora: see Peak-to-Peak Scenic Highway Area. Map E-14

Empire: see Georgetown. Map F-14

ESTES PARK

Includes Drake, Glen Haven and Lyons. Also see Peak-to-Peak
Scenic Highway Area and Loveland. Map: C-14

*Estes Park, a high mountain valley surrounded by snowcapped peaks, is the
gateway community to Rocky Mountain National Park. Downtown, you'll
find mountain gardens and grassy picnic parks, Victorian lights, river walks
and sidewalk benches — old-fashioned charm in a modern community. You
can stuff yourself at one of the fudge shops, browse at one of the many local
gift and craft shops, play golf, sail, ride horseback, hike the backcountry,
enjoy a country show, dine at a first-class restaurant or just plain relax in all
the mountain splendor. There's plenty to see and do, from museums to scenic
drives, fishing to mountain biking — something for everyone.*

Fun Things to Do

- Barleen Family Country Music Dinner Theatre
  Summer: (303) 586-5749; November to April: (602) 982-7991
- Dick's Rock Museum (303)586-4180
- Enos Mills Cabin (303) 586-4706
- Estes Park Golf Course (303) 586-8146, (303) 586-8176
- Moraine Park Visitor Center (303) 586-3777

7 Pines Cabins & Campground

Situated in the spectacular Big Thompson Canyon, these fully furnished, Riverfront cabins sleep two to four people. One cabin has a kitchenette; the two others have fireplaces and an outdoor gas grill for cooking. All three have their own bath. The main house has a bedroom with an outside entrance.

You can fish next to the cabins in the Big Thompson River, or head out to nearby lakes and streams. There are many nearby hiking trails and fine restaurants in downtown Estes Park. Or just relax by a fire and enjoy the breathtaking beauty of the Rockies.

Location: Highway 34, near milepost 70½.

1 housekeeping cabin
2 non-housekeeping cabins
1 lodge room
Camping available
Rates: $$ to $$$

Doug & Marty Walker
2137 Big Thompson Canyon (CB)
Drake CO 80515
(303) 586-3809

Pets: No
Elevation: 7,300
Credit Cards: None
Open May 15 to September 18

Anderson's Wonder View Cottages

These modern cottages and motel, with an outstanding view of the 14,256-foot Long's Peak, are scattered across seven acres of peaceful land next to Rocky Mountain National Park. All units have fireplaces, a private deck and cable television. Each cottage, spaced 50 feet apart for privacy, has a grill and a fully equipped kitchen. Shared facilities include a heated pool, putting green, basketball court, horseshoes, shuffleboard, a picnic area and a playground.

Cabins have a seven-day minimum rental during summer.

Year-round color surrounds the area: spring brings lush green meadows and wildflowers, while summers offer beautiful scenery and cool mountain air. Fall abounds with golden aspen and wildlife, and mild winters showcase one-of-a-kind snowflakes and scenic splendor.

Location: 2½ miles west of downtown Estes Park, ¼ mile north of Highway 36.

10 housekeeping cottages
3 motel rooms with kitchenette
3 motel rooms without kitchenette
Rates: $$$$ to $$$$$

Tom Peter
540 Laurel Lane
P.O. Box 427 (CB)
Estes Park CO 80517-0427
(303) 586-4158
(800) 327-0113

Pets: Yes
Elevation: 8,000
Credit Cards: VM
Open all year

Big Thompson Timberlane Lodge

Located on five acres between Estes Park and Rocky Mountain National Park, Big Thompson Timberlane Lodge has an inspiring view of the Rocky Mountains. It's off the road on the banks of the Big Thompson River, yet within walking distance of restaurants, miniature golf and shopping areas. All of the motel, cottage units and 1,200-square-foot log homes have their own heat, carpeting, cable television with HBO and combination baths or showers. They are available with or without kitchenettes, and the log homes have gas fireplaces. There is a swimming pool and a large hot tub for relaxing after a long day's adventures.

Local activities includes scenic drives to Bear Lake, Fall River Road and Trail Ridge Road.

Location: Highway 36, west of Estes Park.

16 housekeeping cottages
12 motel rooms with kitchenette
5 log homes on the river
1 trailer
Rates: $$ to $$$$$

Curt & Pat Thompson
740 Moraine Ave.
P.O. Box 387 (CB)
Estes Park CO 80517-0387
(303) 586-3137

Pets: No
Elevation: 7,500
Credit Cards: VM
Open all year

Brookside Resort on the River

Here you can find modern cabins and old-fashioned service at affordable prices. The clean, comfortable housekeeping cabins have completely equipped kitchens, linens, dishes, shower-baths and cable television. If you're bringing baby, ask for a crib when checking in. There is a picnic area under pine trees and a private fishing pier on the Big Thompson River. The site is away from traffic and noise, but only 1 mile from Estes Park.

Fish to your heart's content from the resort's private pier. Don't forget your camera when going sightseeing and hiking in nearby Rocky Mountain National Park.

Location: West of town on Riverside Drive, south of Highway 36.

13 housekeeping cabins
3 non-housekeeping cabins
Rates: $$ to $$$$$

Amos & Doris Jean Johnson
725 Riverside Dr.
P.O. Box 1982 (CB)
Estes Park CO 80517-1982
(303) 586-4669

Pets: Yes
Elevation: 7,600
Credit Cards: VM
Open April 1 to November 1

Castle Mountain Lodge on the River

Leave your hectic pace behind for a casual, carefree holiday by the river on 35 acres of pine forest. Castle Mountain's cottages and rooms feature rustic mountain charm, yet have all the modern comforts: color television, outdoor furniture, barbecue, heat, tub and shower-bath and a fully equipped kitchen. Most cabins also have fireplaces. With a restaurant adjacent to the lodge, it's excellent for family vacations, secluded honeymoons and fireside conferences.

Fish in the lodge's well-stocked river, hike in adjacent Rocky Mountain National Park, rent horses from nearby stables or do a little shopping. In the winter, you may see wildlife wandering through the grounds. Your hosts can arrange trail rides, a tee-time at the golf course or dinner theater tickets. In the winter, cross-country ski on National Park trails.

Location: Between Estes Park and Rocky Mountain National Park on Highway 34.

22 housekeeping cottages
7 rooms
Rates: $$$$ to $$$$$

Ruth & Warren Clinton
1520 Fall River Rd. MR (CB)
Estes Park CO 80517-9103
(303) 586-3664
Fax: (303) 586-6060

Pets: Yes
Elevation: 7,500
Credit Cards: VMD
Open all year

Colorado Cottages

This is a place where you're treated like a family guest in true country comfort. Colorado Cottages is a small, intimate spot for getaways, holidays and family vacations at the edge of Rocky Mountain National Park. You'll see lots of wildlife, from birds in the summer to mule deer in the winter. The cottages each have full kitchens, fireplaces, color television and in-room libraries to make you feel at home.

Be sure to inquire about honeymoon, golf, hiking and skiing packages when you call for reservations.

Among the many local activities are fishing, hiking, golf, horseback riding, skiing and snowshoeing. There are shops and restaurants nearby.

Location: On Highway 36, just west of Estes Park on the north side of the road.

11 housekeeping cottages
Rates: $$$ to $$$$

1241 High Dr. MR (CB)
Estes Park CO 80517-9801
(303) 586-4637
(800) 468-1236

Pets: No
Elevation: 7,800
Credit Cards: VMAD
Open all year

Edgewater Heights Cottages

This small, family owned and operated business has clean, cozy cottages at the foot of a pine-covered mountain. Surrounded by the Big Thompson River, where you can catch trout easily, each cottage has one bedroom, a complete kitchen with a microwave oven, a fireplace, color television, dishes and linens.

Go hiking on one of the ground's mountain hiking trails, or barbecue in the shady, spacious picnic area. The cottages are only five minutes from downtown Estes Park, Lake Estes, golf and the fairgrounds.

Location: East of Estes Park on Highway 34, near milepost 66.

8 housekeeping cottages
Rates: $$$

Larry & Debbie McLemore
2550 Big Thompson
P.O. Box 3195 (CB)
Estes Park CO 80517-3195
(303) 586-8493

Pets: No
Elevation: 7,500
Credit Cards: VM
Open May 1 to October 31

Estes Park Center/YMCA of the Rockies

You'll see why four generations of families return to this magnificent setting every year to rejuvenate their bodies, minds and spirits. More than 200 modern housekeeping cabins and 565 lodge rooms are scattered over 860 acres adjoining Rocky Mountain National Park. Each cabin has its own kitchen and private phone; many have fireplaces.

Reservations are required for large groups — the conference and family reunion facilities can accommodate up to 2,500 people.

Depending on the season, bring back vacation memories of hayrides, horseback riding, hiking, indoor swimming, square dancing, miniature golf, tennis, arts and crafts, reading in the library, ice skating, sledding and more. During "SummerFest," view the nearly two dozen fine arts events. The Estes Park Center is just minutes away from the quaint mountain town of Estes Park. Take scenic drives through Big Thompson Canyon, over Trail Ridge Road and the Peak-to-Peak Highway.

Location: West of town on Highway 36. Turn south on Highway 66.

200 housekeeping cabins
565 lodge rooms
Rates: $ to $$$$$

Gary Baxter
2515 Tunnel Rd. (CB)
Estes Park CO 80511-2550
(303) 586-3341

Pets: No
Elevation: 8,010
Credit Cards: None
Open all year

Idlewilde Cottages by the River

These completely equipped cottages are situated in a pine forest on the beautiful Big Thompson River. The one-, two- and three-bedroom cottages have screened porches, cable television and rustic knotty pine interiors. An outdoor hot tub welcomes you home after your mountain adventures. Picnic tables and barbecue grills are ready for your mountain cook-outs after fishing in the Big Thompson River.

This quiet, peaceful setting is only 1 mile from Rocky Mountain National Park. Nearby, you'll find entertainment and shopping in Estes Park. Take your pick of activities: go square dancing, partake in a chuck-wagon dinner and Western shows, or climb a 14,000-foot peak.

Location: Between Estes Park and Rocky Mountain National Park on Highway 66.

13 housekeeping cottages
Rates: $$$$ to $$$$$

Al & Connie Settles
3030 Moraine Rd.(CB)
Estes Park CO 80517-8318
(303) 586-3864
Winter: (303) 651-7846

Pets: No
Elevation: 7,828
Credit Cards: None
Open May 10 to October 15

Inn of Glen Haven

Go back in time at this historic bed and breakfast inn. Faithfully restored to reflect its original charm, this old-world retreat maintains the romantic atmosphere of an intimate English country inn. The rooms are tastefully decorated with antiques, each with its own motif: the colonial George Washington room has a canopy bed, while the Peach Room is decorated in Victorian style with French doors leading to the patio. The two cottages are quiet and secluded, with kitchen and dining areas, bedrooms, private baths and fireplaces. Some of the hotel rooms have two-room suites with a sitting room and a bedroom. While breakfast is included with your stay, you can also enjoy gourmet candlelight dinners and fine wines in the restaurant or pub. After dinner, relax by the huge moss-rock fireplace in the parlor.

Well-behaved children are welcome.

Only 7 miles from Rocky Mountain National Park, the Inn of Glen Haven is off the beaten path, yet is on an all-season highway. In the winter, the Twelve Days of Christmas are celebrated each year with "Old English" feasts.

Location: 7 miles northeast of Estes Park on Devil's Gulch Road.

2 housekeeping cottages
6 historic hotel rooms
Rates: Call for prices

Tom & Sheila Sellers
7468 County Rd. 43 (CB)
P.O. Box 219
Glen Haven CO 80532-0219
(303) 586-3897

Pets: No
Elevation: 7,500
Credit Cards: VM
Open May 1 to February 28

Lazy R Cottages

These sparkling clean cabins with knotty pine interiors look out onto no less than 16 mountain peaks. The cabins, with one, two or three bedrooms, have fully equipped kitchens, color cable televisions, picnic tables and barbecue grills. Many also have fireplaces stocked with free wood. Three new log cabins sleep up to 11 and feature their own private hot tub; the other cabins share a hot tub. After a long morning of hiking, spend a lazy afternoon with your kids at the on-site playground.

Since you'll be close to Rocky Mountain National Park, take advantage of the many recreational opportunities, from driving up Trail Ridge Road to hiking or cross-country skiing in the backcountry.

Location: Highway 36, 1½ miles from Estes Park.

9 housekeeping cabins
1 motel room without kitchenette
Rates: $$$ to $$$$$

Mark Whittlesey, Owner
David Kiser, Manager
891 Moraine Park Rd. (CB)
P.O. Box 1996
Estes Park CO 80517-1996
(303) 586-3708

Pets: No
Elevation: 7,500
Credit Cards: VMD
Open all year

Machin's Cottages in the Pines

You'll discover these deluxe, immaculately clean, beautifully decorated cottages in a secluded location inside Rocky Mountain National Park. Scattered among tall pines and unusual rock formations, the cottages have fully equipped kitchens, fireplaces stocked with free firewood, large picture windows, carpeting, cable color television, porches and patio areas with outdoor furniture and barbecue grills. All linens are provided and exchanged when necessary. And your kids can play happily on the children's playground.

You must stay a minimum of two nights. The owners allow one small pet, but it must remain on a leash. If you're bringing a small child, ask for high-chairs, cribs and bed-rails.

The cottages are near a small Brook and a hiking trail that begins from the property. It's a 1¼-mile hike from your cottage to Beaver Meadows and the spectacular mountain valley of Moraine Park, where other trails spread out into Rocky Mountain National Park. Go fishing in the nearby lake and river, or take a 10-minute drive to Estes Park for dining, shopping and golfing.

Location: Southwest 2½ miles from Estes Park on Highway 36, then go west ½ mile on a side road.

17 housekeeping cottages
Rates: $$$$ to $$$$$

Lee Machin
2450 Eagle Cliff Rd.
P.O. Box 2687 (CB)
Estes Park CO 80517-2687
(303) 586-4276

Pets: Yes (with restrictions)
Elevation: 8,000
Credit Cards: VMA
Open May 20 to October 1

McGregor Mountain Lodge

From this site on the border of Rocky Mountain National Park, you'll gaze over Fall River Canyon to Trail Ridge Road and the Continental Divide. Choose a cozy knotty-pine cottage, a luxury new condominium or an economical room with a kitchenette. The lodge is noted for wildlife: check out the bighorn sheep, hummingbirds and deer. Relax in the hot tub after a day of exploring an entire mountainside or keeping tabs on your kids at the playground.

You can get discounts from September through June. Conference facilities are available for small groups from October through May.

In the spring and summer, enjoy beautiful scenery and wildflowers, hike, play golf, sail, or go horseback riding. In the fall, see aspen trees change to gold, hear the elk bugling and look for bighorn rams butting heads. In the winter, spend cozy evenings by a crackling fire after a sunny day of cross-country skiing, sledding, ice fishing, snowshoeing, or just relaxing in the sun that warms the south-facing slope.

Location: 4 miles west of Estes Park on Highway 34, ½ mile before the entrance to Rocky Mountain National Park near milepost 58½.

22 housekeeping cabins/condos
5 rooms with kitchenette
Rates: $$$$ to $$$$$

Ruth & Warren Clinton
2815 Fall River Rd. MR (CB)
Estes Park CO 80517-9801
(303) 586-3457
Fax: (303) 586-4040

Pets: No
Elevation: 8,000
Credit Cards: VMD
Open all year

National Park Resort Cabins & Campground

Located next to the Fall River entrance to Rocky Mountain National Park on a sheltered, tree-filled mountainside, these housekeeping cabins have fully equipped kitchens, bathrooms with tiled showers, sunken living rooms with fireplaces and color cable television. A delightful climate provides warm, sunny days and cool evenings. With this in mind, the owners provided each cabin with outside tables and chairs, a barbecue grill, a fire ring and wood. For your convenience, the campground has a laundromat, grocery and gift store, small snack bar and a train for the kids. The pine-scented air, blue skies and grand views all help make a great Colorado vacation.

Reservations are required from October through April. You must pay first and last night's deposit; there is a 30-day cancellation policy.

Bordering the National Park, there are hiking trails, fishing, climbing and riding stables close by. The National Park offers a variety of programs, including nature walks, films and evening campfires. Take advantage of the breathtaking views, all within a 20-mile radius. The town of Estes Park, only 5 miles away, has many attractions, restaurants and shops.

Location: 5 miles west of Estes Park at the Fall River entrance to Rocky Mountain National Park on Highway 34.

4 housekeeping cabins
2 motel rooms with kitchenette
3 motel rooms without kitchenette
Camping available
Rates: $$ to $$$$

Dan & Becky Ludlam
3501 Fall River Rd. MR (CB)
Estes Park CO 80517-9801
(303) 586-4563

Pets: Yes
Elevation: 8,300
Credit Cards: VMD
Open May 1 to September 30

Park Place Cabins & Camping Resort

Welcome to a serene part of the Rocky Mountains — here you'll find 35 wooded acres of hillside campsites and comfortably furnished housekeeping cabins, secluded in the Roosevelt National Forest.

Park Place is near both Rocky Mountain National Park and the town of Estes Park for wilderness and civilized vacation activities. Explore trails in the adjacent Roosevelt National Forest by hiking, biking or horseback riding. Swim in the pool, play a game of basketball, have fun at the video arcade, or play horseshoes, among other sports.

Location: 5½ miles southeast of the junction of Highway 34 and 36, near milepost 5.

2 camper cabins
4 housekeeping cabins
Camping available
Rates: $ to $$$

5495 Highway 36
P.O. Box 4608 (CB)
Estes Park CO 80517-4608
(303) 586-4230
(800) 722-2928

Pets: No
Elevation: 7,800
Credit Cards: VMD
Open May 1 to September 30

Rockmount Cottages

Just a mile from the entrance to Rocky Mountain National Park, these scenic cottages by the Big Thompson River are spaced for maximum privacy as well as for the best views. The cottages are decorated with a feeling of mountain lodge ruggedness, while providing modern facilities from kitchen to bath to cable television. All cottages have an outdoor grill and a fireplace, but also have gas heaters for those nippy mornings. There is a centrally located laundromat and game room.

Spacious lawns border the river; you can even climb up Giant Track Mountain in your backyard for a fabulous view of the river valley. Fishing is as close as the river that runs through the resort, with water so clear you can watch the fish take your bait. The cottages border on National Forest land, so you can hike for hours through spectacular scenery.

Location: 2 miles west of Estes Park off of Highway 36 on spur route 66.

15 housekeeping cottages
Rates: Call for prices

Lee & Wanda Apetz
1852 Moraine Route (CB)
Estes Park CO 80517
(303) 586-4168
Winter: (402) 362-6071

Pets: No
Elevation: 7,800
Credit Cards: VM
Open April 1 to December 1

Shelly's Cottages

On the river and off the road on five acres of quiet mountain splendor, these modern, comfortable cottages have private baths, excellent beds with linens, and full kitchens with dishes. Some cottages have fireplaces, while two "special occasion" units have king-sized beds and private hot tubs in their own gazebos. Cook your freshly caught stream trout on the barbecue grills and eat on the shaded picnic tables.

Special occasion packages come with champagne, breakfast baskets, chocolates and dining certificates.

Go for a hike or drive on scenic roads through the high mountain country and dramatic, front range canyons. You are only minutes from fine dining, dinner theaters and the sights of Lyons, Estes Park, Rocky Mountain National Park and Boulder.

Location: 4 miles northwest of Lyons, off of Highway 36 near milepost 16.

9 housekeeping cottages
Rates: $$$ to $$$$$

Pat Kinson
1688 North St. Vrain Dr.
P.O. Box 740 (CB)
Lyons CO 80540-0740
(303) 823-6326
(800) 356-6061

Pets: Yes
Elevation: 6,000
Credit Cards: VMD
Open all year

Timberline Cottages

Although situated in town, these cottages have an out-of-town feeling. With a wide selection of housekeeping cottages nestled in pine trees, Timberline's amenities include cable television, a heated swimming pool, picnic tables and barbecue grills. The cottages are in a hillside setting with a view of Lake Estes and the Front Range.

You're adjacent to restaurants and a grocery store, and you're right across from the Barleens Country Music Theatre. Only ½ mile from downtown Estes Park, you can walk to fairground events, tennis, a public indoor pool and fishing at Lake Estes.

Location: On Highway 7, ½ mile south of downtown on South St. Vrain, near milepost 1.

6 housekeeping cottages
16 motel rooms without kitchenette
Rates: $$$

Herb & Lucy Phelan
P.O. Box 106 (CB)
Estes Park CO 80517-0106
(303) 586-4697
(800) 274-4697

Pets: No
Elevation: 7,570
Credit Cards: VMD
Open May 1 through October 30

Tiny Town Cottages

On 15 acres, with a breathtaking view of the snow-capped peaks of the Continental Divide, these cozy cottages are furnished with everything you need. The one- or two-couple cottages are equipped with fireplaces and free firewood, kitchens, king- or queen-sized beds and color cable television with HBO.

Tiny Town Cottages caters to adults. You must stay a minimum of three nights. To ensure privacy, they do not take large groups or family reunions.

Enjoy a picnic and fish in the adjacent Big Thompson River, or play shuffleboard and horseshoes on the spacious grounds. Tiny Town is close to several fine restaurants, a supermarket and a miniature golf course. The Rocky Mountain National Park, 1 mile away, offers many scenic roads and trails, wildlife, wildflowers and waterfalls in a spectacular mountain setting.

Location: Highway 36, near milepost 5.

19 housekeeping cottages
Rates: $$$

Bob & Helen Mitchell
830 Moraine Ave. (CB)
Estes Park CO 80517-8005
(303) 586-4249

Pets: No
Elevation: 7,644
Credit Cards: VMAD
Open May 1 to October 15

Trails West on the River

These clean and cozy housekeeping cabins are pleasantly situated along the Fall River. All cabins are completely equipped with a fireplace, color cable television, kitchen and private deck or patio. After a day of hiking and touring, relax in the riverside outdoor hot tub. The "Sweetheart Suite" has an in-room hot tub to ensure privacy.

Ask about reserving their new, romantic "special occasion" packages for a memorable stay.

Trails West is located between the town of Estes Park and Rocky Mountain National Park. Local activities include touring, cross-country skiing, fishing, rodeos, chuckwagon suppers, horse shows and square dancing.

Location: Highway 34, near milepost 60.

17 housekeeping cabins
2 motel rooms without kitchenette
Rates: $$$$ to $$$$$

Jeff & Kristin Barker
1710 Fall River Rd. MR (CB)
Estes Park CO 80517
(303) 586-4629

Pets: No
Elevation: 7,500
Credit Cards: VMAD
Open all year

Valhalla Resort

A wide variety of exceptionally clean, comfortable and well-furnished vacation homes, ranging from rustic to luxurious, are tucked away on 11 tree-studded acres next to Rocky Mountain National Park. The cottages are fully equipped with dishes, glassware, pots and pans, coffeemakers and toasters. In the summer, enjoy the swimming pool, while year-round you can soak in the private hot tub or play in the activity center. There is an on-site laundromat and gift shop.

Bring your sweetie for one of the exclusive LoveScapes® vacations, with a private Love Retreat, abundant deli tray, flowers, champagne and other surprises. Valhalla offers senior discounts and special rates during the off-peak season.

Besides the many activities available in Rocky Mountain National Park and the town of Estes Park, Valhalla provides shuffleboard, miniature golf, horseshoes and ping-pong. Bring hiking boots for the trails, a swimming suit for the pool, and warm sweaters for the cool, crisp mountain evenings.

Location: ⅓ mile off Highway 66, near milepost 1, off Highway 36 West.

22 housekeeping cottages
Rates: $$$ to $$$$$

Jim & Ruth Tipton
P.O. Box 1439 (CB)
Estes Park CO 80517-1439
(303) 586-3284

Pets: No
Elevation: 7,700
Credit Cards: VMAD
Open all year

EVERGREEN

Also see Bailey, Denver Area and El Rancho. Map: F-15

Evergreen is nestled in the foothills just 30 miles west of Denver. It offers the quiet beauty and tranquillity of a wooded mountain setting, yet is close to the city for day trips and night life. Old Town Evergreen has unique gifts and specialty shops, antiques and numerous dining opportunities. Nearby Evergreen Lake has ice skating and fishing in the winter; in the summer, you can rent canoes, paddle boats and small sail boats or fish in the well-stocked streams and lakes. There are many nearby parks for picnicking, hiking and mountain biking. Evergreen has easy access for mountain drives to Echo Lake and Mount Evans, Guanella Pass and Fall River Road. Check with the Chamber of Commerce for a list of cultural activities throughout the area.

Fun Things to Do

- Evergreen Golf Course (303) 674-6351
- Hiwan Homestead Museum (303) 674-6262
- International Bell Museum (303) 674-3422

Bauer's Spruce Island Chalets

Bauer's Spruce Island Chalets on 19 acres provides comfort and convenience throughout the year. All chalets have living rooms, bathrooms, shower-tubs and from one to four bedrooms. The large chalets have fireplaces and cable television. Most surround a large lawn, where you can barbecue, picnic and play lawn games, including croquet and badminton.

Walk along Cub Creek or fish in the property's small pond. Public park lands to the east are easily accessible for hiking and fishing. In addition, take your pick of stores, craft shops, fishing, churches, restaurants, art galleries, golf, horseback riding stables and tennis courts. If you want solitude, drive to the nearby scenic areas where you can watch wildlife and birds frolic on the mountainside.

Location: From Highway 74, go through Burgan Park to Evergreen. Turn west on Highway 73, then turn south on Brook Forest Road.

6 housekeeping chalets
Rates: $$$ to $$$$$

Paul & Maureen Harrison
5987 S Brook Forest Rd.
P.O. Box 1678 (CB)
Evergreen CO 80439-1678
(303) 674-4757

Pets: No
Elevation: 7,200
Credit Cards: VMAD
Open all year

Davidson Lodge Cabins on a Stream

Half an hour west of Denver in the mountains along beautiful Bear Creek, Davidson's four log cabins are divided into two separate units, each ideal for a couple or small family. The cabins have knotty pine interiors, gas ranges, refrigerators, modern bathrooms, large wood-burning fireplaces and cable television. They also supply all dishes, cooking utensils, linens, blankets and towels.

Central City with its summer festivals, opera house and casinos, is only a short drive west. Evergreen has churches, restaurants, gold courses and riding stables nearby. An hour's drive will take you to either Loveland or Berthoud Pass, with dramatic, panoramic views of the top of the continent and excellent downhill skiing. Or drive to Georgetown, with its historic buildings, Georgetown Loop Narrow Gauge Steam Train and silver mine tour. Delightfully cool evenings, the crackling fire on the hearth, the sound of the hurrying stream and the clean mountain air all make a memorable, relaxing vacation.

Location: ½ miles east of Evergreen on Highway 74, near milepost 8.

9 housekeeping cabins
Rates: $$$$

Patty & Ron Aufmuth
27400 Highway 74 (CB)
Evergreen CO 80439-5804
(303) 674-3442

Pets: No
Elevation: 7000
Credit Cards: VMA
Open all year

Evergreen Lodge

These beautifully furnished cabins are beside a creek, nestled among towering blue spruce trees. The cabins have fully equipped kitchens, microwave ovens, cable televisions, large fluffy towels, comfortable beds and gourmet coffee and tea. Some cabins have fireplaces with free wood. There is also a lovely creek-side picnic area with barbecue grills.

You can hike and fish in the forests of Evergreen, or go to town, where you can play golf, dance, ice skate on the lake in winter, shop and dine in fine restaurants. If you like gambling or a bit of history, take a bus from Evergreen to the casinos in Central City and Blackhawk. Ski to your heart's content at nearby Summit County ski resorts. Take a short drive to Denver for a day at the zoo or to partake in the many downtown cultural events.

Location: At Highway 73 and Brookforest Road, 1 mile south of the dam on Highway 7, on the southwest side of the road.

8 housekeeping cabins
Rates: $$$$

Coral Carley
5331 Highway 73
P.O. Box 2861 (CB)
Evergreen CO 80439-2861
(303) 674-6927

Pets: No
Elevation: 7,500
Credit Cards: VM
Open all year

Highland Haven Resort Cottages

Set amid spectacular rock outcroppings, towering evergreens and the scenic Bear Creek, Highland Haven is in one of Colorado's most exquisite settings, yet only one block east of downtown Evergreen. Tasteful landscaping, a flowered arbor and a charming fountain complement a variety of distinctive accommodations. Stay by the fireplace in a cozy cottage or a spacious suite, or relax in a delightful motel room. The Gardener's Cottage is a special cabin with a canopy bed made from willow branches, a moss-rock fireplace, antique furnishings, a private deck overlooking Bear Creek and a Jacuzzi. All rooms have fully equipped kitchens, linens and towels.

Some of Colorado's best skiing is less than an hour away, at Winter Park, Keystone, Loveland or Copper Mountain. If you prefer, cross-country ski in the surrounding backcountry, or go ice skating and ice fishing on Evergreen Lake. Explore the town of Evergreen, venture to Denver, or drive west into the mountains and old mining towns. Be sure to ask your hosts about having your silhouette cut by Patti Rose, one of America's finest free-hand silhouette artists.

Location: Highway 74, near milepost 7.

10 housekeeping cottages
2 non-housekeeping cottages
4 motel rooms without kitchenettes
Rates: $$$ to $$$$$

Tom Statzell & Gail Riley
4395 Independence Trail S (CB)
Evergreen CO 80439-8516
(303) 674-3577
(303) 674-0346

Pets: Yes
Elevation: 7,000
Credit Cards: VMAD
Open all year

GEORGETOWN

Includes Empire. Map: F-14

Once the third-largest town in Colorado, Georgetown is full of restored Victorian homes and buildings, making it an exceptional National Historic District. With its easy access off Interstate 70, this is a great tourist stop. While the town itself has many fine restaurants and gift shops, there are ghost towns and old mine ruins scattered throughout the canyons and mountains. The Georgetown Loop Narrow Gauge Steam Train makes a complete spiral as it climbs the steep canyon above the town. Other steam trains run excursions up to Silver Plume during the summer. Nearby is the not-to-be-missed-world's highest paved road to the top of Mount Evans. Arapaho National Forest attracts outdoor enthusiasts for its great hiking, cross-country skiing, 14,000-foot peaks, snowmobile trails and downhill skiing in the Loveland area.

Fun Things to Do

- Georgetown Loop Railroad (303) 670-1686
- Hamill House (303) 674-2625
- Hotel De Paris (303) 569-2311
- Silver Plume School House (303) 569-2145

The Peck House

Built in 1860, this is the oldest hotel still operating in Colorado. The 11 guest rooms are filled with period antiques, many that Mrs. Peck shipped by ox-cart from Chicago. Mr. Peck saw the same stunning valley views when he arrived in 1859 to pan for gold. The Peck House hotel registry features the signatures of P.T. Barnum, Ulysses S. Grant and General Sherman. Be sure to dine at the five-star Signature Restaurant for more old-town ambiance. Although abundant with history, the Peck House owners did concede to modern lifestyles — they added a plant-filled spa room that accommodates 12.

The Empire valley offers many activities, including searching out old mining trails, mountain biking and four-wheel driving, horseback riding and gallery browsing. The Peck House is at the gateway to many major ski areas and Rocky Mountain National Park. Check with your hosts for local concerts and tour schedules for museums and the Georgetown Loop Narrow Gauge Steam Train. It's a short drive to the historic district and gambling casinos in Blackhawk and Central City.

Location: 2 miles west of I-70 (exit 232) on Highway 40.

11 historic hotel rooms
Rates: $$$$ to $$$$$

Gary & Sally St. Clair
83 Sunny Ave.
P.O. Box 428 (CB)
Empire CO 80438
(303) 569-9870

Pets: No
Elevation: 8,600
Credit Cards: VMA
Open all year

Thee Victorian Village Tourist Cottages

Step back into an era when hospitality was an art and elegance was a way of life. Quaint cottages for two are surrounded by panoramic views. Each cottage has a small, furnished kitchen, a breakfast nook, a microwave oven and color television. Relax in the shared hot tub or in front of a gas log fireplace after a day's activities. Great for honeymooners and weekend getaways.

Smoking is not permitted in the cabins.

Enjoy year-round outdoor activities: fishing, hiking, skiing, photography and much more. The Victorian Village is near the Georgetown Loop historic narrow-gauge railroad and the ski areas of Winter Park, Berthoud Pass and Loveland.

Location: On the north edge of Empire. From Highway I-70, take exit 232.

4 housekeeping cottages
Rates: $$$$ to $$$$$

Phil Fisher, Owner
Carol Jensen, Manager
148 W Park Ave.
P.O. Box 134 (CB)
Empire CO 80438-0134
(303) 433-1369
Reservations: (800) 395-1955

Pets: No
Elevation: 8,600
Credit Cards: VMD
Open all year

Glen Haven: see Estes Park. Map: C-15

GLENWOOD SPRINGS

Includes New Castle. Map: G-7

From the days when the Ute Indians camped at the hot springs, to the late 1800s when New Yorkers and Europeans flocked to the Spring's healing warmth, Glenwood Springs has been a popular and affordable vacation spot. Nestled in a valley of pine-covered mountains, this area offers warm summer days with plenty of activities, from whitewater rafting to hiking and bicycling. Glenwood Springs is a winter wonderland, with activities such as downhill and cross-country skiing, snowmobiling — even dogsledding and innertubing. The Hot Springs pool is said to be the world's largest outdoor mineral pool, larger than a football field and relaxing in any season.

Fun Things to Do

- Frontier Historical Society & Museum (303) 945-4448
- Glenwood Springs Golf Course (303) 945-7086
- Hot Springs Pool (303) 945-6571
- New Castle Historical Society (303) 984-2926 (private residence)
- Rifle Creek Golf Course (Rifle) (303) 625-1093
- Rock Gardens Rafting (303) 945-6737
- Silt Historical Park (303) 876-2668 or (303) 876-2702
- Westbank Ranch Golf Course (303) 945-7032

Ami's Acres Camper Cabins & Campground

The owners call it "a Rocky Mountain experience." Bring your own bedding to these camper cabins for an economical way to see the many sights of the Glenwood Springs area. The campground has picnic tables and a laundromat for your convenience.

The area has enough activities to fill your entire vacation: take a dip in the Glenwood Springs Hot Springs pool, go downhill or cross-country skiing, hike the many trails, play golf, take a horseback ride, dine in fine restaurants, or fish and hunt while enjoying the spectacular scenery.

Location: 3½ miles out of town. Take exit 114 from I-70, then go west 1 mile on Frontage Road.

2 camper cabins
Camping available
Rates: $

Paul & Jacqueline Amichaux
50235 Highway 6 & 24
P.O. Box 1239 (CB)
Glenwood Springs CO 81602-1239
(303) 945-5340

Pets: No
Elevation: 5,700
Credit Cards: VM
Open March 15 to November 15

Hideout Cabins & Campground

These rustic, secluded and quiet cabins, near Glenwood Hot Springs and the Roaring Fork River, have kitchens with dishes, television, linens and fireplaces in some rooms. There is also a laundromat and a game room on the premises.

Recreation is endless. Visit the world's largest hot springs pool, play golf and dine in Glenwood Springs' fine restaurants. Ski nearby slopes, such as Sunlight, Snowmass and Aspen. Hike or horseback ride in Hanging Lake and Flat Tops, or fish the Colorado, Roaring Fork and Frying Pan rivers. Raft the wild Colorado, spelunk in the Cave of Clouds and Hubbard, and visit Doc Holliday's grave.

Location: Exit 116 off of I-70, 2 miles south of Glenwood Springs. Off of Highway 82, near milepost 2, on Four Mile Road.

12 housekeeping cabins
Camping available
Rates: $$ to $$$$$

Gary & Debbie Morley
1293 Rd. 117 (Four Mile Rd.) (CB)
Glenwood Springs CO 81601
(303) 945-5621

Pets: No
Elevation: 5,800
Credit Cards: VMAD
Open all year

Knotty Pine Lodge

Across from the Roaring Fork River, come relax and enjoy the Rocky Mountains from the modern cabins and lodge rooms at Knotty Pine Lodge. Units include fully equipped kitchenettes, cable television and complete laundromat facilities. The cabins surround a park-like setting for barbecuing, lawn games and lounging.

Ask about their special ski packages and group rates.

Be sure to relax in the Glenwood Springs Hot Springs pool between shopping, fishing, hunting and skiing — Aspen, Sunlight, and Snowmass ski areas are just a few miles away.

Location: Exit 116 off I-70, 2 miles south on Highway 82.

18 housekeeping cabins
4 lodge rooms
Rates: $$$

William & Lee Hill
2706 Grand Ave. (CB)
Glenwood Springs CO 81601-4426
(303) 945-6446
(800) 726-5940

Pets: Yes
Elevation: 5,728
Credit Cards: VMAD
Open all year

New Castle/Glenwood Springs KOA & Kamping Kabins™

Bring your own bedding supplies and cooking utensils for their camper cabins, located on a trout-stocked mountain creek, surrounded by woods and high mountain peaks. If you don't already have them, they sell fishing and hunting licenses. Eat at the Creekside Cafe or order the food service and picnic in the spacious group area from Memorial Day to Labor Day.

Each Saturday, enjoy the cowboy steak barbecues. The New Castle/Glenwood Springs KOA is an excellent base camp for nearby attractions and activities, including mountain climbing, hiking, wind surfing, rafting, horse rides and both miniature and regular golf courses.

Location: 2½ miles north of New Castle, 9 miles west of Glenwood Springs. Off of I-70, at exit 105.

6 camper cabins
Camping available
Rates: $$

0581 County Rd. 241 (CB)
New Castle CO 81647
(303) 984-2240

Pets: Yes
Elevation: 6,000
Credit Cards: VM
Open May 7 to October 30

Ponderosa Lodge

Join in the 50-year-old tradition of feeding cracked corn and apples to the deer that appear each winter at the rustic log cabins and contemporary A-frames, nestled among the oldest trees in Glenwood Springs. These quiet, cozy cabins have kitchens, fireplaces and cable television, with HBO, Cinemax and Showtime. Picnic in the two-acre fenced park behind the cabins, or play volleyball and horseshoes in the family playground.

The Ponderosa Lodge is near the famous Glenwood Springs Hot Springs pool and various activities, such as fishing, rafting, fine dining, spelunking in the vapor caves, sightseeing, golfing, horseback riding, skiing and hunting.

Location: On Frontage Road off I-70, near exit 114.

17 housekeeping cabins
Rates: $$$ to $$$$$

Ray & Carla Johnson
51793 Highway 6 & 24 (CB)
Glenwood Springs CO 81601
(303) 945-5058

Pets: Yes
Elevation: 6,500
Credit Cards: VMAD
Open all year

Riverside Cottages

At the southern city limits of Glenwood Springs, this heavenly wooded 4½-acre site has a 1,200-foot frontage on the Roaring Fork River. The cottages accommodate up to 12 people, and have modern kitchens, cable television, private bedrooms and linens — and maid service daily! Some cottages have fireplaces with furnished wood. For those who like barbecuing, there are plenty of grills, picnic tables and lawn chairs.

Although they encourage reservations, they welcome drive-in visitors when space is available.

The Roaring Fork River is stocked with trout for excellent fishing year-round. Your hosts can arrange rafting, hunting trips and sightseeing trips if necessary.

Location: At the southern city limits of Glenwood Springs off of Highway 82.

15 housekeeping cottages
Rates: $$$ to $$$$$

Henry & Lillie Govone
1287 County Rd. 154 (CB)
Glenwood Springs CO 81601
(303) 945-5509

Pets: No
Elevation: 5,700
Credit Cards: VMA
Open all year

Spruce Tree Ranch

These modern log cabins are in a magnificent, quiet setting, with views of high mountain peaks and lovely wooded areas. A beautiful creek flows past each cabin. Although you can't cook in the cabins, you can barbecue that freshly caught trout on the outside grills in front of your cabin. Kids also love the playground.

This photographer's paradise features wildlife, birds, flowers and snow-capped mountains. Visit the Rifle Gap Reservoir and the unusual Rifle Falls. Hike in the Flat Tops Wilderness area, fish in streams and reservoirs, hunt, ride a horse, raft the Colorado River, or just relax by the stream. And don't forget the famous Glenwood Springs Hot Springs pool to ease the sore muscles after a day of adventure.

Location: 2 miles northwest of New Castle, I-70 Exit 105.

5 non-housekeeping cabins
Rates: $$

Ralph & Elaine Lindstrom
2026 Rd. 245 (CB)
New Castle CO 81647
(303) 984-2144

Pets: No
Elevation: 5,900
Credit Cards: None
Open May 1 to November 15

Golden: see Denver Area. Map: F-16

GOULD

Includes Cowdrey, Rand, and Walden. Map: B-12

Gould is situated at the west end of the scenic Poudre Canyon, west from Fort Collins on Highway 14. The major recreational activity in this area is fishing for Brown or Rainbow trout — the Cache La Poudre River offers long stretches of accessible water along its rush east from the high mountains of Rocky Mountain National Park. In addition, the area has popular hiking trails and four-wheel drive roads. Nearby Cameron Pass has excellent cross-country skiing, snowshoeing and snowboarding for the more adventurous.

Fun Things to Do

North Park Pioneer Museum, Walden (303) 723-4711

Seven Utes Mountain Lodge, Motel, Cabins & RV Park

This lodge, built in the 1920s, now includes rustic non-housekeeping cabins, modern motel units and lodge rooms. The main lodge has a cozy lounge, a restaurant that serves delightful Western food, a sauna and a beer garden. There's also a wilderness chapel for weddings and religious retreats right on the premises.

The lodge is 4 miles west of Cameron Pass between the Medicine Bow Mountains and the Never Summer Range, so you'll find a lot to do in this sparsely populated area. The Roosevelt National Forest and Rawah Wilderness areas have four-wheel drive trails and hunting and fishing opportunities. You can go cross-country skiing on well-groomed trails or rent horses and mountain bikes from the lodge — you may even see a moose while you ride through the scenic mountain trails.

Location: 4 miles west of Cameron Pass on Highway 14, near milepost 61; 70 miles west of Fort Collins.

6 non-housekeeping cabins
4 motel rooms without kitchenette
3 historic lodge rooms
Camping available
Rates: $$ to $$$

Loren Maxey
61014 Highway 14 (CB)
Walden CO 80480-9521
(303) 723-4368

Pets: Yes
Elevation: 9,433
Credit Cards: VM
Open all year

Whistling Elk Ranch

Enjoy being "city slickers" for a day on this 7,000-acre, 40-year-old working cattle ranch in North Park where you'll help with cattle drives and branding. Their deluxe, modern cabins feature full kitchens and bathrooms, wood-burning fireplaces and electric heat. In the evening, gaze at stars from the secluded outdoor hot tub after "working" all day.

The ranch sponsors a "backcountry camp," where you ride in by horseback or mountain bike and spend the night under a blanket of stars. The morning greets you with a breathtaking view of Parkview Mountain and the smell of a delicious Western breakfast. Fish in the 3 miles of private stream or stocked pond. Explore the ranch's many trails, either on a gentle horse, on foot, your mountain bike, or by cross-country skis. Photograph wildlife, including elk, mule deer, black bear, moose, coyotes and eagles, or ask the ranch about guided big-game hunts.

Location: 90 miles west of Fort Collins on Highway 14, near milepost 51.

3 housekeeping cabins
Rates: $$$$ to $$$$$

Verl Brown & John Ziegman
P.O. Box 2 (CB)
Rand CO 80473
(303) 723-8311

Pets: No
Elevation: 8,600
Credit Cards: No
Open all year

Granby: see Grand Lake. Map: D-13

Grand Junction: see Grand Mesa Area. Map: H-2.

GRAND LAKE

Includes Granby. Also see Rand. Map: D-13

Grand Lake is a mountain hideaway for year-round vacationing. The village maintains a rustic charm, complete with board sidewalks, yet provides modern amenities of dining and shopping. Located at the west entrance to Rocky Mountain National Park and surrounded by Arapaho National Forest on the shores of Grand Lake, this village has everything you can imagine in its breathtaking scenery. Grand Lake offers plenty of activities: horseback riding, boating, hiking, live theater, golfing and river rafting. When the snow starts in mid-October, Grand Lake becomes a winter playground, with groomed trails for snowmobiling, cross-country skiing and snowshoeing. The village is surrounded by towering peaks, high mountain lakes, rushing streams, rivers and waterfalls. Granby, in Colorado's spectacular middle park, sports downhill skiing in the winter and a variety of summer mountain activities, from mountain biking, river rafting, boating and fishing to llama trekking.

Fun Things to Do

- Grand Lake Golf Course (303) 627-8008
- Kaufman House (303) 627-3351
- Klein's Fishing Lodge (303) 887-3507, (303) 887-3209
- Lake Shore Marina (303) 887-2295, (303) 421-0060 off season
- Norton Marina (303) 887-3456
- Hot Sulphur Springs Mineral Baths and Pool (303) 725-3306

Antler's Cabins

These rustic housekeeping cabins are grouped around a water fountain near Grand Lake, Colorado's largest natural lake. Each cabin has a full kitchen or kitchenette with dishes and small appliances, shower bathrooms, a living/dining room with a hide-a-bed couch, cable television with HBO, private bedrooms and picnic areas. You can reserve the conference cabin for group meetings or workshops.

There are year-round activities close to Grand Lake: in the winter, look for downhill and cross-country skiing, skating and sledding; in the summer, enjoy hiking, horseback riding, fishing, swimming, tennis, golf, boating and mountain biking. You can even rent motor scooters to zip around the scenic areas.

Location: ½ block south of Grand Avenue on Broadway.

7 housekeeping cabins
Rates: Call for prices

Robert & Susan Latham
450 Broadway
P.O. Box 1200 (CB)
Grand Lake CO 80447-1200
(303) 627-8012

Pets: No
Elevation: 8,300
Credit Cards: VM
Open all year

Beacon Landing Motel & Marina

Beacon Landing offers rustic, secluded units overlooking picturesque Lake Granby in the Arapaho National Forest, near the entrance to Rocky Mountain National Park. The Cabaña is a two-bedroom mobile home with a screened-in front porch and wood stove, while the Beach House cabins, which can accommodate up to nine people, have fully equipped kitchens and rock fireplaces. All units are furnished with linens, cooking utensils and dishes, and each has an individual porch, barbecue grill and color television. For convenience, there's also a recreation room and a small country store with food, snacks, bait, rental equipment and hunting and fishing licenses.

At the marina, rent guided fishing and pleasure boats during the summer. In the winter, ask your hosts about snowmobile trips and ice taxi service. Be sure to visit scenic areas, including the National Forest and Rocky Mountain National Park.

Location: Northwest of Highway 34, near milepost 10.

1 housekeeping cabin
7 motel rooms with kitchenette
1 trailer for rent
Rates: $$ to $$$$$

David & Jane McCloskey
P.O. Box 590 (CB)
Granby CO 80446-0590
(303) 627-3671
(800) 864-4372

Pets: Yes
Elevation: 8,300
Credit Cards: VMAD
Open all year

Kickapoo Lodge

These three- to five-room, well-spaced cottages are surrounded by trees on Shadow Mountain Lake and Grand Lake. They are quiet, yet within walking distance of town. The cottages are completely equipped and furnished with every comfort and convenience for housekeeping, including refrigerators. Each also has central heating and cable television.

The lodge requires a one-week minimum stay and recommends reservations. For those without private transportation, your hosts can meet you at the Amtrak station in Granby, or you can take a shuttle from the Denver airport.

For guests who bring their boats, the lodge offers a private boat landing. Also enjoy the other activities in the Grand Lake area — as the Western Gateway to Rocky Mountain National Park, there are 50 peaks over 10,000 feet high to photograph or climb.

Location: South of town, off of Highway 34, near milepost 15.

6 housekeeping cottages
Rates: $$

Dorothy Young
1100 Jerico Rd.
P.O. Box 486 (CB)
Grand Lake CO 80447-0486
(303) 627-3369

Pets: Yes
Elevation: 8,369
Credit Cards: None
Open June 1 to October 1

Mountain Lakes Lodge

"The only thing we overlook is the Continental Divide," your hosts often say. Located on a canal that joins Lake Granby with Shadow Mountain Lake and Grand Lake, you'll notice clusters of cabins and log houses for multiple-sized groups. All cabins have fully equipped kitchens and linens. Depending on cabin size, amenities include cable television, fireplaces and private decks with wonderful mountain views. There are even miniature log cabins in the playground area for the kids.

The west entrance to Rocky Mountain National Park is only minutes away. The many outdoor activities during the summer and winter months include hiking, fishing in lakes or the canal, photography, boating, cross-country and downhill skiing and snowmobiling at nearby Winter Park and Silver Creek. Check out the abundant small wildlife, from chipmunks and squirrels to hummingbirds.

Location: Highway 34, near milepost 10.

13 housekeeping cabins
Rates: $$ to $$$$$

Mike Farragher
10480 Highway 34
P.O. Box 160 (CB)
Grand Lake CO 80447-0160
(303) 627-8448

Pets: Yes (no cats)
Elevation: 8,300
Credit Cards: None
Open all year

Rapids Lodge

Built in the early 1900s on the banks of the Tonahutu River, Rapids Lodge has a rustic atmosphere with modern comforts. Located away from town by the river in a quiet, wooded area, the historic lodge rooms feature four-poster beds with dust-ruffled quilts, clawfoot bathtubs and cable television. If you want more modern amenities, try their new condominiums; most of these variable-sized units have kitchens, but if not, the restaurant serves elegant candlelit dinners.

Take a ride in a horse-drawn buggy or stagecoach into town, play 18 holes of golf, attend live theater shows, enjoy a sunset boat tour on the lake, fish outside your door in the Tonahutu River or visit the high country of Rocky Mountain National Park.

Location: On the east edge of town.

3 housekeeping cabins
10 condominium units
8 historic hotel rooms
Rates: Call for prices

Lou & Toni Nigro
209 Rapids Lane
P.O. Box 1400 (CB)
Grand Lake CO 80447-1400
(303) 627-3707

Pets: No
Elevation: 8,500
Credit Cards: VMAD
Open all year

Shadow Mountain Ranch & Resort

This ranch puts the best of the mountain area's ambiance at your doorstep. Make yourself at home in private cabins, with kitchenettes for doing your own cooking or, if you feel sociable, join in on the popular and delicious group meals. The lodge is a good place for workshops, entertainment or just plain conversation in a comfortable atmosphere.

The Shadow Mountain Ranch & Resort is near Rocky Mountain National Park and Lake Granby for hunting, fishing, boating and hiking.

Location: 5½ miles north of Highway 40 on Highway 125, near milepost 5.

6 housekeeping cabins
Rates: Call for prices

Jacque Spacek
P.O. Box 963 (CB)
Granby CO 80446-0963
(303) 887-9524

Pets: Yes
Elevation: 8,000
Credit Cards: VM
Open all year

Shadowcliff Lodge & Cabins

On a beautiful cliffside setting, Shadowcliff Lodge overlooks Grand Lake, with the roaring North Inlet Stream flowing by on the east side. The nine sleeping rooms with common bathrooms, and the dormitory rooms, which serve as an internationally registered youth hostel, share the first-floor lounge, kitchen and dining area. Three cabins with fireplaces are set apart from the lodge alongside a rushing mountain stream. You can eat three nutritious and inexpensive meals every day, including specially baked fresh bread. The on-site Shadowcliff Chapel provides a beautiful worship setting and doubles as a meeting area for retreats, religious conferences, seminars, workshops and family reunions.

Ask about group accommodations and rates.

Nearby activities include horseback riding, boating, fishing, hiking, rafting and attending live theater productions. The lodge is adjacent to Rocky Mountain National Park, Arapaho National Forest and Indian Peaks Wilderness areas.

Location: Take Highway 34 to Grand Lake Village, near milepost 15. Entering town, take Left Fork on West Portal Road and continue ¾ mile. Turn left at the Shadowcliff sign.

3 housekeeping cabins
19 lodge rooms
14 dormitory beds
Rates: $ to $$$

Warren, Patt, Peter & Karen Rempel
405 Summerland Park Rd.
P.O. Box 658 (CB)
Grand Lake CO 80447-0658
(303) 627-9220

Pets: No
Elevation: 8,500
Credit Cards: None
Open June 1 to September 30

Winding River Mountain Resort

This health resort satisfies your every need for relaxation — an indoor pool, sauna, whirlpool, steam, salon and massage center. The modern cabins are fully carpeted and include fireplaces. In the large dining room, eat family-style, wholesome foods, such as homemade breads and desserts, fresh salads, vegetables, fruits, fish, chicken, turkey, lamb and beef.

Reserve your cabin for either the American or bed and breakfast plan. You can also reserve space for your horse — there are private pens, riding arenas, a beautiful barn and spectacular riding areas. In the summer, you may even want to take a dressage clinic.

Choose from a myriad of nearby activities: horseback riding, cross-country skiing, golfing and fishing.

Location: Northeast of Grand Lake off of Highway 34.

4 non-housekeeping cabins
Rates: $$$$$

Bob & Elaine Busse
1471 County Rd. 49
P.O. Box 629 (CB)
Grand Lake CO 80447-0650
(303) 627-3251

Pets: Yes
Elevation: 8,600
Credit Cards: None
Open all year

Winding River Resort Village

Located on 160 wooded acres, this family-run resort borders Rocky Mountain National Park. You can reserve quaint, one-bedroom cabins in the pines or lodge/bed and breakfast rooms, named Trapper, Molly Brown and Americana. Breakfast really is a gourmet feast, featuring country sausage or bacon, creative egg dishes, fresh fruits, pancakes or waffles and fresh-ground coffee.

Advanced reservations are required.

The Winding River Resort Village sponsors many activities, such as horseback riding, pony rides, hayride steak dinners, sleigh rides, a Frisbee golf course, chuckwagon breakfasts, ice cream socials and an animal farm for kids. Spend an evening around the campfire enjoying a chuckwagon supper and a cowboy musical show. Nearby sports include mountain biking, hiking, horseback riding, cross-country skiing, snowmobiling and more.

Location: Take Highway 34 to Kawuneeche Visitor Center north of Grand Lake. Turn west on 491 and go 1½ miles northwest.

2 housekeeping cabins
3 lodge or bed and breakfast rooms
Camping available
Rates: $$$$ to $$$$$

Wes & Sue House
1447 Road 491
P.O. Box 629 (CB)
Grand Lake CO 80447-0629
(303) 627-3215
Denver area: (303) 623-1121
(800) 282-5121

Pets: Yes (deposit required)
Elevation: 8,700
Credit Cards: VMD
Open all year

GRAND MESA AREA

Includes Cedaredge, Grand Junction and Mesa.
Also see Delta and Paonia. Map: I-5

Grand Mesa, with an expanse of 53 miles, is the largest flat-top mountain in the world. As you travel across Grand Mesa, you'll see forests of aspen and spruce, flowered meadows and over 200 cool clear lakes offering fantastic fishing for Rainbow, Brook, natives and Brown trout. You can reach many of the lakes from the highway, but for the more adventurous, there are some lakes only accessible by four-wheel drive, by foot or by horseback. Abundant wildlife makes Grand Mesa a popular area for fall hunting. In the winter, with an average of 30 feet of snow, you can enjoy ice fishing, snowmobiling and cross-country skiing. Escape the hustle of everyday life and relax in Grand Mesa's pure mountain air.

Fun Things to Do

- Alexander Lake Lodge Restaurant (303) 856-6700
- Colorado National Monument, Fruita (303) 858-3617
- Cross Orchards Living History Farm, Grand Junction (303) 434-9814
- Deer Creek Village Golf Course, Grand Junction (303) 856-7781
- Dinosaur Valley, Grand Junction (303) 243-DINO
- Doo Zoo Children's Museum, Grand Junction (303) 241-5225
- Electric Mountain Lodge Restaurant (303) 929-5522
- Grand Mesa Lodge Store & Gift Shop (800) 551-MESA
- Lincoln Park Golf Course, Grand Junction (303) 242-6394
- Mesa Lakes Restaurant (303) 268-5467
- Museum of Western Colorado, Grand Junction (303) 242-0971
- Surface Creek Historical Society Pioneer Town, Cedaredge (303) 856-3006
- Tiara Rado Golf Course, Grand Junction (303) 245-8085
- Western Colorado Center for the Arts, Grand Junction (303) 243-7337

Alexander Lake Lodge & Campground

Vacation on top of the world at over 10,000 feet in the landmark of Grand Mesa. Built at the turn of the century from local materials, including an enormous fireplace said to contain 200 tons of rock, the historic lodge overlooks Alexander Lake and Twin Lakes. All housekeeping cabins feature modern amenities with a rustic ambiance. The lodge dining room serves memorable meals during regular hours every day. The lodge store sells groceries and all the supplies you'll need for your nearby fishing or big-game hunting trips.

Hiking and sightseeing are a must in this area. Ride horses, hike, snowmobile and cross-country ski to the 280 lakes in the area. Or hunt the abundant deer and elk that proliferate Grand Mesa.

Location: In Grand Mesa National Forest, 2 miles east of Highway 65, near milepost 27.

3 housekeeping cabins
3 non-housekeeping cabins
Camping available
Rates: $$$ to $$$$

Gordon & Grace Nelson, Owners
Judy Fawcett, Manager
2121 AA 50 Rd.
P.O. Box 900 (CB)
Cedaredge CO 81413-0900
(303) 856-6700

Pets: No
Elevation: 10,2000
Credit Cards: VM
Open all year

Electric Mountain Lodge

In the heart of the Gunnison National Forest, the historic Electric Mountain Lodge has comfortable lodge and dormitory rooms. After your day in the forest, unwind in the spacious hot tub, take in the beautiful views from the restaurant or relax by the fireplace in the large lounge while watching satellite television.

Rent your choice of transportation to ride the Sunlight to Powderhorn Trail: horseback, mountain bike or snowmobile. The lodge offers snow-cat tours, or ask about the excellent fishing, hunting and hiking in this area.

Location: From Highway 133 near milepost 36, go north 18½ miles on Stephens Gulch Road.

10 lodge rooms
19 dormitory beds
Rates: $$$$

Debbie Lynch & Will Byrd
2880 4010 Drive
P.O. Box 370 (CB)
Paonia CO 81428-0370
(303) 929-5522

Pets: No
Elevation: 9,200
Credit Cards: VM
Open all year

G R Bar Ranch Cabins

If you've dreamed about an exciting trip, this is it. The secluded, G R Bar Ranch Cabins are nestled between elevations from 7,200 to 11,000 feet, adjoining both the Gunnison and Grand Mesa National Forests. You rent these completely furnished cabins by the week, so you can really settle into a vacation away from it all.

Call ahead if you don't have a four-wheel drive. Your hosts will meet you in Paonia and take you to the ranch.

Take advantage of unlimited fishing in seven private lakes — and you won't need a license. Explore thousands of nearby acres by horseback, jeep or on hiking trails. You're in the center of nature's wonderland, with scenic views, myriads of wildflowers, wildlife, deer and elk — a photographer's delight.

Location: Off Highway 133 at Paonia.

3 housekeeping cabins
Rates: call for prices

N.W. & Barbara Grosse-Rhode
4149 N80 Lane (CB)
Paonia CO 81428-9639
(303) 527-6434

Pets: No
Elevation: 9,500
Credit Cards: None
Open May 15 to November 1

Grand Mesa Lodge

In Grand Mesa National Forest, 55 miles from Grand Junction, you'll find cozy housekeeping cabins and a motel above beautiful Island Lake. These attractively furnished log cabins have fully equipped kitchens, gas heat and bathrooms with showers. A comfortable lobby has a scenic view for relaxation, conversation and coffee. Shop in the on-site store for groceries, gifts, antiques, authentic Indian jewelry, fishing and hunting supplies, including licenses.

Island Lake is the largest lake on Grand Mesa, and outstanding mile long and surrounded by evergreens and aspen trees — you can rent boats at the lodge or fish to your heart's content. Nearby you'll find horseback riding and excellent restaurants.

Location: Highway 65, near milepost 28.

14 housekeeping cabins
2 motel rooms without kitchenette
Rates: $$ to $$$

Chuck & Jan Harrington
P.O. Box 49 (CB)
Cedaredge CO 81413-0049
(303) 856-3250;
(800) 551-MESA

Pets: Yes
Elevation: 10,500
Credit Cards: VM
Open May 15 to October 30

Mesa Lakes Resort

Breathe the cleanest air around! High on fabulous Grand Mesa, surrounded by forests and lakes, Mesa Lakes Resort offers various rustic to modern vacation cabins. Bring your own cooking utensils; some rooms have kitchenettes. A small, on-site grocery store also sells hunting and fishing licenses. And enjoy the delicious homemade bread, pies, chili and cinnamon rolls in the lodge's restaurant.

Mesa Lakes Resort is nestled among seven of the finest of these lakes, all within walking distance of the cabins. More than 200 lakes in the area provide great fishing and boating opportunities. Hike, hunt for deer and elk or photograph the wondrous scenery and wildlife.

Location: 14 miles south of Mesa, off of Highway 65, near milepost 36.

4 housekeeping cabins
8 non-housekeeping cabins
3 motel rooms without kitchenette
Rates: $$ to $$$$$

Sally & Amy Henderson
P.O. Box 230 (CB)
Mesa CO 81643-0230
(303) 268-5467
Home: (303) 434-2795

Pets: No
Elevation: 9,800
Credit Cards: VM
Open May 15 to November 5

Granite: see Twin Lakes. Map: I-12

Great Sand Dunes National Monument: see Alamosa and Antonito. Map: N-14

Green Mountain Reservoir: see Summit County. Map: E-11

GUNNISON

Includes Almont, Parlin and Sargents. Also see Crested Butte.
Map: K-9

Gunnison is nestled in the broad Gunnison River Valley, home of Western State College, centrally located for some of Colorado's finest recreation. Enjoy 2,000 miles of trout streams, or partake in the exciting boating and fishing on the state's largest lake, Blue Mesa Reservoir. There's plenty to see and do, from fly-fishing lessons to four-wheel drive rentals, golf to ghost towns, historic walking tours, ice fishing and ice skating, llama pack trips, mountain biking and museums, rafting, sailing and skiing, snowmobling, tramway rides, water-skiing and windsurfing. No doubt about it — you'll pack in a lifetime of memories while visiting this area.

Fun Things to Do

- Curecanti National Recreational Area (303) 641-2337
- Dos Rios Golf Course (303) 641-1482
- Monarch Valley Horse Rides, Fishing and Restaurant (800) 869-9455, (303) 641-6177
- Pioneer Museum (303) 641-9963 or (303) 641-0943
- Three Rivers Outfitting, Rafting & Willow Fly Anglers (303) 641-1303

7-11 Ranch

The Rudibaugh family has hosted outdoor experiences at this ranch, situated on Quartz Creek and surrounded by majestic mountains, for 30 years. Their semi-rustic cabins have fully equipped kitchenettes with a stove and a private bathroom.

You can fish for dinner in one of the many native trout streams right outside your cabin door or in the ranch's stocked private pond. Take part in their yearly cattle drive, where you can be a cowhand, helping 800 head of cattle over a 12,000-foot pass into their summer pasture. You'll camp under the stars and join the other cowhands for meals served by the camp cook. Locally, you can choose from a myriad of horseback trips, from day-long outings to five- or seven-day pack trips in some of the most beautiful scenery in Colorado. Your hosts also can help outfit your hunting trip for big horn sheep, elk and mule deer.

Location: 5 miles north of Highway 50 on County Road 76.

5 housekeeping cabins
Rates: Call for prices

Rudy Rudibaugh
5291 County Road 76 (CB)
Parlin CO 81239
(303) 641-0666

Pets: No
Elevation: 8,500
Credit Cards: None
Open May 22 to September 1

Ferro's Trading Post

Spend your summer vacation in a relaxing atmosphere amid a natural setting of forest, lakes and streams. Overlooking Blue Mesa Reservoir, these cabins, which accommodate up to six people, have complete kitchens with all utensils and linens. For your convenience, there's a laundromat, and the trading post sells groceries, gas, liquor, propane and fishing and hunting licenses.

Be sure to ask about special vacation packages with boat tours and trail rides or, if you're an experienced hunter, check out the "drop camps" and guided hunting trips. Bring your horse to ride the trails, then board it directly on the premises during the evening. Also enjoy the barbecues and barn hoedowns during special occasions. Ferro's Trading Post is surrounded by the Gunnison National Forest, so there are ample opportunities for hiking, four-wheel driving and horseback riding.

Location: Take Highway 50, exit Lake Fork Entrance. Go north 0.7-mile past the dam. Turn right on Soap Creek Road.

4 housekeeping cabins
8 dorm rooms
2 RVs for rent
Camping available
Rates: $$

Kay & John Ferro
3200 Soap Creek Rd.
P.O. Box 853 (CB)
Gunnison CO 81230-0853
(303) 641-4671

Pets: Yes
Elevation: 7,800
Credit Cards: VM
Open May 1 to November 30

Granite Mountain Lodge & Outfitters

Granite Mountain Lodge offers week-long trips filled with high-country wilderness adventure. Spend three nights in the rustic lodge, one night at a high mountain camp, then ride horseback over the continental divide and raft down through the whitewater of Brown's Canyon.

Location: 13 miles north of Highway 50, near milepost 190, close to the small town of Sargents, on County Road 888, Tomichi Creek Road (partly paved).

15 lodge rooms
Rates: Call for prices

Susan B. & Don Glittenberg
County Road 888, Tomichi Creek Rd.
P.O. Box 10 (CB)
Sargents CO 81248
Summer: (719) 539-2303
Off-season: (817) 627-7993

Pets: Yes
Elevation: 10,300
Credit Cards: None
Open June 1 to September 5

Lonesome Coyote Enterprises/JMB Ranch

For a true "get away from it all" vacation, JMB Ranch is hard to beat. Located on a private ranch next to the Gunnison National Forest and the West Elk Wilderness area, these cabins are secluded, private and rustic.

Reservations are required; during winter and spring, you must reserve two months in advance. You're also welcome to board your horses here.

In the winter, cross-country ski in one of the most beautiful and remote parts of the state. There is also excellent, seasonal hunting among the area's abundant elk and deer.

Location: 25 miles northwest of Gunnison on FR 730.

2 housekeeping cabins
Rates: $$$$$

Frank & Marlys Buffington
3148 County Road 730 (CB)
Gunnison CO 81230
(303) 641-2433

Pets: No
Elevation: 9,100
Credit Cards: None
Open all year

Lost Canyon Resort

In a beautiful, 10-acre location overlooking the Gunnison River in a peaceful and grassy setting, Lost Canyon Resort log cabins are modern and fully equipped with private bathrooms and kitchens with ranges, refrigerators, dishes and cookware. With accommodations that can sleep up to eight people, the resort also supplies all bed linens, blankets, soap and towels. Many cabins offer fireplaces or wood stoves. To really get away from the hustle and bustle of the city, the rooms have no televisions or telephones.

The Central Gunnison country location is ideal for hunting, skiing and fishing — this is the only resort on the Gold Medal section of the Gunnison River, close to three reservoirs and many smaller rivers and streams. You can downhill or cross-country ski, ice fish and snowmobile in the Crested Butte ski area, only 20 miles away.

Location: 8 miles north of Gunnison, just east of Highway 135, near milepost 8.

17 housekeeping cabins
Rates: $$$ to $$$$

Bob & Catherine Reinhardt
8264 Highway 135 (CB)
Gunnison CO 81230-9620
(303) 641-0181

Pets: Yes
Elevation: 8,000
Credit Cards: VM
Open all year

Monarch Valley Ranch

Surrounded by snow-capped peaks of the Rocky Mountains, Monarch Valley Ranch is a real working ranch. The Tomichi River roars through the ranch, feeding into private trout lakes. After a day's hiking or skiing, relax your sore muscles in one of their soothing hot tubs. The lodge also has a redwood deck where you can sit and enjoy that first cup of coffee. Your family will never leave hungry from the Grub House restaurant, where all meals are served daily. Load up with supplies in the on-site sporting goods and grocery stores.

Ride one of the ranch horses to the Continental Divide, where natural lakes offer fishing in dramatic mountain scenery. Fish for trout in the river or in one of their private lakes. Participate in world-record elk hunting among the 3.7 million acres of the Gunnison and Rio Grande National Forests, both adjacent to the ranch. For downhill ski enthusiasts, Monarch Pass ski area is known for its deep powder runs and short lift lines, while the Crested Butte ski area is ranked one of the best in the country. Cross-country skiers will find numerous trails in the forests and surrounding areas.

Location: Highway 50, near milepost 185, 5 miles west of the Continental Divide, 25 miles east of Gunnison.

2 housekeeping cabins
22 lodge rooms
Camping available
Rates: Call for prices

Shannon & Kim Atkisson
67366 Highway 50 E. (CB)
Gunnison CO 81230-9401
(303) 641-6177
(800) 869-9455

Pets: Yes
Elevation: 8,500
Credit Cards: VM
Open all year

QT Corner Store & Cabins

If you really want to get away from the rat race, Parlin is about as small and remote a town as you'll find in the Rocky Mountains, with a population of 46. QT's clean, modern kitchenette cabins are ideal for a quiet, do-nothing-but-enjoy-yourself vacation — you'll have ample opportunities for eating, sleeping, drinking, walking and reading.

Cast your fishing rod in Quartz Creek as it flows past Parlin or head up Quartz Creek to Ohio, Pitkin, the Cumberland Pass, Tincup, Taylor Park and the rest of the west.

Location: Highway 50, near milepost 169.

5 housekeeping cabins
Rates: Call for prices

Chuck & Earl Glaze
1 Earl Avenue
P.O. Box 1 (CB)
Parlin CO 81239-0001
(303) 641-0485

Pets: Yes
Elevation: 7,980
Credit Cards: None
Open June 1 to November 15

Rockey River Resort

This ranch, homesteaded in 1892, features old and new log cabins on the Gunnison River, with fully equipped kitchens and fireplaces or wood stoves for your light housekeeping needs. They provide all blankets, bed linens, towels, cooking utensils, dishes and flatware.

If necessary, call ahead so your hosts can meet you at the Gunnison airport or bus terminal and bring you to their resort.

The abundant beauty of this country is unmatched. All of nature's colors in rocks and mountain flowers are displayed throughout the many scenic circle trips designed for your enjoyment. Check out a bit of history in the many ghost towns, old mines and relics. If you're more interested in sporting activities, Rocky River Resort is within easy access to hunting, lake fishing, skiing, rafting and horseback riding.

Location: 6 miles north of town, ½ mile east of Highway 135, near milepost 6.

14 housekeeping cabins
Camping available
Rates: $$$

Joe Marvel
4359 Country Rd. 10 (CB)
Gunnison CO 81230-9606
(303) 641-0174

Pets: Yes
Elevation: 7,860
Credit Cards: VMA
Open all year

Shady Island Resort, Cabins & RV Park

This resort, situated on the banks of the Gunnison River, features housekeeping cabins ranging in size from one-room to a large three-bedroom cabin, with a living room, dining room and kitchen. All cabins have a shower or tub and a kitchen or kitchenette. Some include fireplaces. The resort also has a playground and miniature golf course.

Ask your hosts about organized raft trips and tubing on the Gunnison River.

Shady Island Resort is conveniently close to Gunnison, within 2 miles of a shopping center, service station and laundromat. Enjoy fishing in the Gunnison River or on the many other nearby lakes and streams.

Location: Highway 135, 2½ miles north of Gunnison, near milepost 3.

10 housekeeping cabins
Camping available
Rates: $$

Arlie & Odessa Griffith
2776 North Highway 135 (CB)
Gunnison CO 81230-9705
(303) 641-0416

Pets: Yes
Elevation: 7,810
Credit Cards: VMD
Open April 15 to November 1

Silent Spring Resort

Two rustic-style, fully modern log cabins with well-equipped kitchens are located in beautiful Spring Creek Canyon, surrounded by National Forest. The resort offers quiet, peace and privacy to visitors who desire a secluded but comfortable setting. The small cabin sleeps three; the large cabin sleeps six and includes a fireplace with free wood. All cabins come with bedding, towels, cooking and eating utensils, refrigerators, gas stoves and showers.

Try out the excellent fishing on Spring Creek and the Taylor River and other reservoirs and streams close by. Make reservations for raft trips, horseback rides, hayrides and pack trips from nearby Harmel's. You can also golf on two 18-hole courses just 30 minutes away.

Location: Go 18 miles north of Gunnison on Highway 135, near milepost 10. Turn east at Almont on Taylor River Road (FR 742) to Harmel's; then go 1 mile up Spring Creek Road.

2 housekeeping cabins
4 RV sites available
Rates: $$$$

Robert & Dorothy Stringer
912 County Rd. 744
P.O. Box 405 (CB)
Almont CO 81210-0405
July to August: (303) 641-2989
September to June: (909) 924-9387

Pets: No
Elevation: 8,453
Credit Cards: No
Open July 1 to September 4

Three Rivers Resort

Named for the Taylor, East and Gunnison Rivers in the heart of the Gunnison National Forest, the Three Rivers Resort features private, rustic and modern riverfront cabins with fully equipped kitchens. Some contain fireplaces and full bath facilities; others retain the Old West atmosphere with a nearby central bath. The pavilion, which accommodates up to 100 people, features pool, foosball and many table games — ideal for family reunions. Other on-site facilities include a laundromat, a general store and a professional fly and tackle shop.

In the summer, join in the many resort-sponsored activities, including square dances, bingo and potlucks. The resort also offers mild or wild raft and inflatable kayak trips — raft down scenic Taylor Canyon and to areas only accessible by boat. Hike and backpack in the National Forest to immerse yourself in the clear streams, lakes, wildflowers, rocks, forests and wildlife.

Location: 10 miles north of Gunnison in Almont, on Highway 135 near milepost 10.

27 housekeeping cabins
Camping available
Rates: $$$

Mark & Mary Jo Schumacher
130 County Rd. 742
P.O. Box 339 (CB)
Almont CO 81210-0339
(303) 641-1303

Pets: Yes
Elevation: 8,000
Credit Cards: VMAD
Open April 15 to November 15

GYPSUM

Including Wolcott. Map: F-9

Located between Vail and Aspen, Gypsum is a gateway to the unspoiled White River National Forest, home to the largest elk herd in North America. Clear streams, born in sky-touching, snow-capped mountains, flow through wildflower meadows and into blue mountain lakes. Here, you can enjoy many scenic and exciting moments rafting, fishing and skiing among the wildlife and rare birds.

Golden Eagle Ranch

This 160-acre, high-country ranch is located in the White River National Forest. The log cabins stand on the edges of mountain meadows amid colorful aspen and blue spruce. The cabins, which sleep from two to five people, are nestled next to one of three clear mountain streams.

Advance reservations are required.

Bill Walden, a professional sculptor, offers roomy, sunlit studio space and instruction for all ages. Bring your own art supplies or purchase them at the studio. Take some time to fish for the abundant Brook, Rainbow and Cutthroat trout in the ranch's lake and beaver ponds. Fishing and boating enthusiasts will enjoy Lede Reservoir, just 2 miles away. Hikers will want to strike out for many of the high lakes in the surrounding mountains. Bring your camera: this is the place to spot Golden Eagles, Red-tailed Hawks, and elk and deer. Venture to Glenwood Springs Hot Springs pool or go whitewater rafting on the Colorado River.

Location: 16 miles south of Gypsum on a county-maintained road.

1 housekeeping cabin
2 non-housekeeping cabins
Rates: $$$ to $$$$$

Bill & Linda Walden
P.O. Box 833 (CB)
Gypsum CO 81637-0833
(303) 524-9311

Pets: No
Elevation: 8,500
Credit Cards: No
Open all year

Wolcott Inn

This bed and breakfast on the Eagle River has a dining- living-room that doubles as a breakfast area and conference room. The inn has a private stretch of river for fishing.

Ask your hosts to book dog sled rides and balloon rides or privately guided cross-country skiing tours. The Wolcott Inn is close to many activities, including raft trips, fly fishing, hunting, hiking and biking. In the winter, cross-country ski, snowmobile and snowshoe in nearby ski resorts, including Beaver Creek, Arrowhead and Vail. Guided cross-country ski tours are provided by the inn.

Location: At the junction of Highway 6 and Highway 131.

6 bed and breakfast rooms
Rates: $$$

Tim Farley & Jan Joulflas
P.O. Box 5 (CB)
Wolcott CO 81655-0005
(303) 926-5463
(303)926-3402

Pets: No
Elevation: 6,960
Credit Cards: VM
Open all year

Hahn's Peak: see Steamboat Springs. Map: B-9

Hovenweep National Monument: see Dolores. Map: O-1

HOWARD

Also see Coaldale and Salida. Map: K-13

Located in the heart of the Arkansas River Canyon, this area is best known for its outstanding whitewater rafting. There are more than 70 licensed rafting outfitters in the Upper Arkansas Valley, offering a variety of trips and services. If you're looking for a less-adventurous experience, you can fish for trout in specially designated areas or in the multitude of mountain streams and lakes, where you'll find smaller Brook, Cutthroat and Rainbow trout. There's ample opportunity for four-wheel drive trips, hiking and horseback riding. Howard is a small community offering the opportunity to relax and get away from it all!

Sugarbush Rustic Housekeeping Cabins & Campground

These rustic housekeeping cabins are an excellent base camp for seeing South Central Colorado. Sugarbush is tucked into tall pines near the Arkansas River, with a striking view of the Twin Sisters peaks. All guests use the central restrooms and showers. Other amenities include a covered pavilion for group activities and reunions, a game room and laundromat. In the eclectic and well-stocked general store, you'll find antique tractors on display and a surprising range of unusual collectibles, antiques and souvenirs for sale.

Fish and watch the deer from the ¼-mile frontage on the Arkansas River or relax by the small Brook that runs through the campground. Nearby, you'll find excellent fishing, rafting, horseback riding and hiking on the many breathtaking trails, after which you can dine at one of the many restaurants in the area.

Location: 12 miles east of Salida, 35 miles west of Royal Gorge, on Highway 50, near milepost 235.

4 housekeeping cabins
Camping available
Rates: $$ to $$$

Bill & Sandy Tunstall
9229 Highway 50 (CB)
Howard CO 81233
(719) 942-3363
(719) 942-3325

Pets: Yes
Elevation: 6,815
Credit Cards: VM
Open April to November

Keystone: see Summit County. Map: F-13

LAKE CITY

Map: M-7

Lake City, 250 miles from Denver, is central to a wide-range of mountain activities. Take a Jeep ride over Engineer Mountain or boat on Lake San Cristobal, one of Colorado's largest natural lakes. Fish for Rainbow trout in the swirling Lake Fork River or explore the Victorian charm of downtown Lake City, Colorado's largest historical district, with over 75 buildings from the late 1800s.

Fun Things to Do

- Hinsdale County Historical Museum (303) 944-2515
- National Historic District (303) 944-2527
- Rocky Mountain Jeep Rental (303) 944-2262
- Gwendolyn's Art Gallery (303) 944-2641

Castle Lakes Campground Resort & Cabins

This resort, nicely situated in a remote, quiet 45-acre aspen and spruce forest, features fully furnished cabins designed for light housekeeping. Barbecue in the outside cook and picnic areas by day; relax around a campfire in the evening. The on-site recreation room has a fireplace, pool table and a play area for children.

The high-altitude valley, surrounded by mountains, has two private fishing lakes (no state license required). You can also fish in the area's many lakes and streams, climb to the tops of nearby 14,000-foot peaks or rent horses and four-wheel drive vehicles to traverse into the remote areas. Try the nationally designated Scenic Alpine Loop over Cinnamon Pass, returning over Engineer Pass, or head to the famous ghost towns in nearby Carson.

Location: Highway 149, near milepost 72. Go 2½ miles south of Lake City, then 7½ miles above Lake San Cristobal on Cinnamon Pass Road. Stay to the right.

3 housekeeping cabins
4 trailers for rent
Camping available
Rates: $$ to $$$

Dick & Mary-Lee Cooper
P.O. Box 909 (CB)
Lake City CO 81235-0909
(303) 944-2622

Pets: Yes
Elevation: 9,200
Credit Cards: No
Open May 15 to October 1

Cinnamon Inn Bed & Breakfast/Gwendolyn's Art Gallery

Built in 1878 as a home for a local jeweler, this converted, well-appointed bed and breakfast inn has the elegance of a Victorian home and the grace of a bygone era. The unique guest rooms and suites have individual Victorian decoration and furnishings, each in a different style, named after famous Lake City residents. Those who want some modern amenities will find a whirlpool tub in the Kitty Eastman suite. To start your morning, your friendly, hospitable hosts serve a delicious gourmet country breakfast. Stick around for afternoon lemonade and sun-tea on the back porch. When evening rolls around, choose from several public rooms to gather around the piano, read or play a variety of games.

Visit the nearby natural wonders: hike to the summits of 14,000-foot peaks, picnic in alpine meadows, sail on Lake San Cristobal or fish in mountain streams. In the winter, snowmobile and downhill or cross-country ski close by.

Location: In town on Highway 149, near milepost 72.

4 bed and breakfast rooms
Rates: $$$$ to $$$$$

Mel & Gwendolyn Faber
426 Gunnison Ave.
P.O. Box 553 (CB)
Lake City CO 81235-0553
(303) 944-2641

Pets: No
Elevation: 8,675
Credit Cards: VM
Open all year

Built in 1878

Crystal Lodge

Tucked away in the trees off the main highway, Crystal Lodge lives up to its motto: "A treat and a retreat." With tasteful, immaculate accommodations, the cottages have two bedrooms, a living room, completely furnished kitchen and full bath. The adjoining apartments all have their own kitchen and full bath, while the lodge rooms have one double bed or two twin beds and a private shower-bath. All accommodations get clean towels daily and fresh linens weekly. Fine foods, prepared from scratch in their kitchen, are served in the charming restaurant. For those warmer days, take a dip in the on-site heated swimming pool.

The Crystal Lodge may be 300 miles from the nearest freeway, but it's right next to nature at its best. Hiking and cross-country ski trails begin at the front door. Lake and stream fishing is just a stone's throw away. Nearby, you can rent horses or a Jeep and escape into the high country — the San Juan Mountains offer a spectacular range of high peaks, pristine lakes, abundant wildlife and picturesque relics of the Gold Rush.

Location: Highway 149, near milepost 70.

4 housekeeping cottages
5 apartments with kitchenette
9 lodge rooms
Rates: $$$ to $$$$$

Gale & Ann Udell
Highway 149 S
P.O. Box 246 (CB)
Lake City CO 81235-0246
Summer: (303) 944-2201
(800) 984-1234
FAX (303) 944-2503

Pets: Yes (approval required)
Elevation: 8,700
Credit Cards: No
Open all year

Moncrief Mountain Ranch

Nestled in the foothills of the San Juan Mountains of Southwestern Colorado, Moncrief Mountain Ranch provides visitors with a uniquely enchanting group vacation spot. The 19,300-square-foot log cabin lodge is an impressive retreat on 320 acres of aspen-covered mountain slopes. A 28-foot-high fireplace dominates the main lounge area, which is surrounded by French windows that offer spectacular views of 14,000-foot peaks and the Lake Fork Valley. A stairway travels up each side of the fireplace to the eight private rooms and two dormitory-style wings on the top floor. Each room is individually decorated and depending on the room, sleep from one to eight people. The wings sleep 14 or more. There are also two dormitory-style cabins that each sleep up to 24 people. The Carson View Grill provides a free breakfast; for other meals, choose from appetizing Southwestern dishes or, after catching trout in the private pond, you can barbecue them on the large, outdoor grill. If you're anxious to see your photographic scenes immediately, you can develop your own prints in the complete black-and-white darkroom. Relax in the outdoor hot tub after a hard day's adventures, or plan group activities for the 100-seat auditorium.

It's just a short hike to the Continental Divide, Diamond Falls and the Rock Slide, a geological point of interest.

Location: On Highway 149, turn east on County Road 30 past the lake where the paved road ends. Go 1.8 miles.

8 lodge rooms
2 dormitories
Rates: $$$ to $$$$$

Blain Moncrief
County Rd. 30
P.O. Box 593 (CB)
Lake City CO 81235-0593
(303) 944-2796

Pets: Yes
Elevation: 9,100
Credit Cards: VM
Open May 15 to October 31

Old Carson Inn

Named after a nearby old mining camp, this large, country log home is filled with antiques and collectibles. Each guest room, named after local mines, is decorated in an individual style. All rooms have private baths and share a large common area filled with games, books and a satellite television. Relax in the enclosed sun porch and view the abundant wildlife, or soak in the hot tub after an active day. The dining room serves outstanding country breakfasts, featuring homemade bread, rolls and sourdough specialties.

The inn, located on a National Backcountry Byway, features ghost towns, jeeping, fishing, mountain biking and hiking on the area's five "fourteeners." During the fall, enjoy the area's fabulous autumn colors or take advantage of excellent deer and elk hunting. In the winter, try out the groomed snowmobile trails and scenic cross-country ski trails.

Location: Off Highway 149, near milepost 72. Go 8 miles south on Cinnamon Pass Road (the Alpine Loop), then 4 miles above Lake San Cristobal.

6 bed and breakfast lodge rooms
Rates: $$$ to $$$$$

Don & Judy Berry
7801 County Rd. 30
P.O. Box 144 (CB)
Lake City CO 81235-0144
(303) 944-2511

Pets: No
Elevation: 9,200
Credit Cards: VM
Open May 1 to March 1

Pleasant View Resort & Rocky Mountain Jeep Rental

These completely modern and fully equipped housekeeping cabins with queen-sized beds and cable television are at the south end of town. There is a large playground for children.

Trek the hiking trails starting at your doorstep or rent a new Jeep for a scenic ride through the beautiful San Juan Mountains. Visit Silverton, Ouray or the old abandoned mining towns in Carson.

Location: Highway 149, near milepost 72.

9 housekeeping cabins
Rates: $$$$

Juanell & Jim Skinner
P.O. Box 174 (CB)
Lake City CO 81235-0174
(303) 944-2262

Pets: No
Elevation: 8,671
Credit Cards: VMD
Open May 1 to October 31

Ryan's Roost

Located high in the San Juan Mountains of Southwestern Colorado, this lovely country home features bed and breakfast rooms and housekeeping cabins. The bed and breakfast rooms with private baths are decorated in an attractive country style, including fireplaces. The "High Lonesome" log cabin accommodates up to eight and has a den, loft, kitchen, laundromat room, two bedrooms and two bathrooms. The "Cliff House" is smaller, with two bedrooms and one bath. Both cabins have decks with spectacular views.

There is a five-day minimum stay. Reserve corral space for your horse at no extra charge. Smoking is permitted in the cabins and on the decks of the main house.

Ryan's Roost is close to everything in the Lake Fork Valley, including fishing in the Lake Fork of the Gunnison River and Lake San Cristobal, the second largest natural lake in Colorado, hiking in the National Forest, climbing 14,000-foot peaks, four-wheel driving over the Alpine Loop, hunting deer and elk, cross-country skiing and snowmobiling.

Location: Highway 149, near milepost 81, 8½ miles north of Lake City.

2 housekeeping cabins
3 lodge or bed and breakfast rooms
Rates: $$$ to $$$$$

Therese & Jim Ryan
9501 Highway 149
P.O. Box 218 (CB)
Lake City CO 81235-0218
(303) 944-2339

Pets: Yes (in cabins only)
Elevation: 8,681
Credit Cards: VM
Open all year

Texan Resort Cabins

Established in 1946 on the banks of the Lake Fork of the Gunnison River, this resort features a beach and a 65-foot waterfall. The comfortable log cabins are set in a wooded hollow among tall spruce, fir, aspen and cottonwood trees, surrounded by large green lawns. All of the cabins have modern plumbing with showers or tubs and completely equipped kitchens. Some have fireplaces or wood stoves. Your hosts supply all linens and towels. There are several barbecue areas to grill your favorite meal.

Enjoy the traditional, resort-sponsored Thursday night cookouts. They also offer guided snowmobile tours in the winter, generally from Thanksgiving through March or early April, but fishing season is year round. Jeeping on the hundreds of miles of the old 1890s mining trails takes you to exciting new vistas and remote fishing locations. Lake San Cristobal is just 2½ miles from your door, while dozens of other smaller lakes are nearby.

Location: Highway 149, near milepost 71. South of Lake City on County Road 142.

15 housekeeping cabins
Camping available
Rates: $$ to $$$

Steve & Gayle Meredith
P.O. Box 156 (CB)
Lake City CO 81235-0156
(303) 944-2246

Pets: No
Elevation: 8,671
Credit Cards: No
Open all year

Westwood Resort

Westwood Resort welcomes you to private one- or two-bedroom cabins, perfect for the rustic mountain retreat or fun family getaways. Each cabin is furnished with queen-sized beds, color televisions, fully equipped kitchens, large refrigerators (to hold all of those fish you'll catch) and unlimited mountain air.

Reservations are recommended — every seventh night is free.

You're sure to enjoy Lake City and the surrounding area. Walk where the prospectors risked everything pursuing the elusive Mother Lodes. Climb 14,000-foot peaks, explore the San Juan Mountains by four-wheel drive vehicles or mountain bikes, fish the lakes and streams for trout, or simply enjoy the beautiful vistas you won't find in any city. And as for crisp, clear nights…when was the last time you saw the Milky Way?

Location: In town on Highway 149, near milepost 72.

8 housekeeping cabins
Rates: $$$$

Glenn & Barbara Lohn
P.O. Box 278 (CB)
Lake City CO 81235-0278
(303) 944-2205

Pets: Yes
Elevation: 8,671
Credit Cards: VMAD
Open May 1 to November 1

Woodlake Park

Near the Alpine Loop Scenic Byway, Woodlake Park has two "bunkhouse" camper cabins, with a double bed and a bunk bed. There is an outdoor grill and picnic table, but you supply bedding, lantern and cooking utensils. A luxury cabin facing the Lake Fork of the Gunnison river accommodates up to 10 in its two bedrooms and on sofa sleepers in the living room. There is a full bath downstairs and a half bath upstairs between the bedrooms. The kitchen features all-new appliances and a dining area.

Enjoy the river and mountain scenery on the covered porch or partake in the organized, fun pavilion activities. There's no end of exciting adventures in the area: birdwatching, fishing, and visiting the many geological interests and old ghost towns.

Location: 2½ miles south of Lake City on Highway 149, near milepost 69.

2 camper cabins
1 housekeeping cabin
Camping available
Rates: Call for prices

Latellya Smith
Highway 149 South
P.O. Box 400 (CB)
Lake City Co 81235-0400
(303) 944-2283
Off-season: (817) 536-4079

Pets: Yes
Elevation: 9,000
Credit Cards: No
Open June 1 to September 30

LAKE GEORGE

Includes Tarryall Reservoir. Map: I-15

Lake George was founded in 1887 when a Boston manufacturer, George Frost, built a dam at the mouth of Elevenmile Canyon. The town of Lake George was built a few miles away. Workers cut ice from Lake George to refrigerate railroad boxcars that contained vegetables and fruit. A nearby attraction, the Florissant Fossil Beds, contains one of the world's largest natural collections of fossil plants and insects — more than 80,000 specimens have been removed from the Florissant lake bed. Eleven Mile State Recreation Area offers fishing, boating, sailing, and hunting. Gem hunters can find geothite, amazonite, and smoky quartz in the area northeast of Lake George.

Fun Things to Do

- Florissant Fossil Beds National Monument (303) 748-3253
- Eleven Mile State Park (719) 748-3401

Eleven Mile Motel Cabins

Located in the town of Lake George, Eleven Mile Motel Cabins are surrounded by the Pike National Forest. Some of these modern, comfortable log cabins have kitchens; all have cable television, carpets, modern bathrooms with showers and great views of the Tarryall Mountain Range.

The Pike National Forest, only ¼ mile away, is known for its scenic beauty, horseback riding, hiking, biking, stream and lake fishing and rock hunting. You'll be only 22 miles from Cripple Creek, with its historic buildings and casinos. Fish in the South Platte River or in nearby Eleven Mile, Spinny, Tarryall and Antero Reservoirs. Visit the famous Royal Gorge and the Florissant Fossil Beds National Monument.

Location: In town on Highway 24, near milepost 267.

8 housekeeping cabins
2 motel rooms without kitchenette
Rates: $$ to $$$$

Tom & Pat Brown
38122 Highway 24 (CB)
Lake George CO 80827
(719) 748-3931

Pets: Yes (with deposit)
Elevation: 8,100
Credit Cards: VM
Open all year

Platte River Cabins & Campground

The cozy Platte River Cabins offer affordable, non-housekeeping cabins and campsites for your whole family.

Gamble at Cripple Creek or fish, hunt and boat in the heart of the Rockies. Nearby, visit Eleven Mile Reservoir, surrounded by Pike National Forest.

Location: On Highway 24, near milepost 265, 40 miles west of Colorado Springs.

7 housekeeping cabins
Camping available
Rates: $$$

John & Christi Hasbun
8966 County Rd. 90 (CB)
Lake George CO 80827
(719) 748-3822

Pets: Yes
Elevation: 8,000
Credit Cards: VM
Open all year

Ute Trail River Resort

Several comfortable log cabins are situated on the Tarryall River in the scenic Rocky Mountains. Each cabin, which can house up to four people, has a fully equipped kitchenette, including pans, dishes and utensils. You bring your own towels, washcloths and soap. For your convenience, choose between a central shower-house or private bathrooms. The facilities can accommodate up to 45 people for groups and family gatherings. An on-site store furnishes your incidental needs.

The resort has its own section of the Tarryall River — be sure to take advantage of the daily fly-fishing instruction. This is a very scenic area, with hiking, rock hunting and bird watching. You can fish in the river and in Tarryall Reservoir only 4 miles away and hunt in the forested areas during big game season.

Location: From Highway 24, go 1 mile west of Lake George. Take Tarryall Road (County Road 77) for 23 miles. From Highway 285 at Jefferson, take City Road 77 for 24 miles.

8 housekeeping cabins
Rates: $$ to $$$

Ronald & Nila Green
21446 County Rd. 77
P.O. Box 159 (CB)
Lake George CO 80827-0159
(719) 748-3015

Pets: Yes
Elevation: 8,900
Credit Cards: VM
Open April 15 to November 30

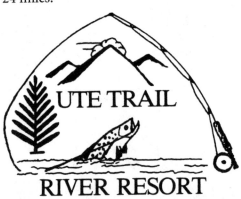

Lake San Isabel: see Rye. Map: M-17

LEADVILLE

Also see Twin Lakes. Map: H-12

Leadville is a jewel in the crown of Colorado history. Silver mining turned Leadville into a boisterous, bawdy boom town overnight — the scent of easy money brought all types to the high Rockies. No visit to Leadville is complete without a journey into the town's history. Learn the tragedy of Baby Doe and see how Horace Tabor became Colorado's Silver King. The Leadville area is also alive with recreational activities. Throughout the year, you'll be awestruck at the two highest peaks in Colorado, Mt. Elbert and Mt. Massive, both over 14,400 feet high. Throughout the summer, tour the San Isabel National Forest or enjoy fishing in the miles of trout streams, hiking, biking, camping, golfing, four-wheel driving, horseback riding, rockhounding and gold panning. During the winter, ski downhill and cross-country or snowmobile in the wide open spaces. And in the fall, you'll want to bring your camera to capture the aspens ablaze with color.

Fun Things to Do

- Heritage Museum & Gallery (719) 486-1878
- Historic Home of H.A.W. Tabor (719) 486-0551
- Leadville Colorado & Southern Railroad (719) 486-3936
- Matchless Mine Museum (719) 486-0371
- Mt. Massive Golf Course (303) 486-2176
- National Mining Hall of Fame & Museum (719) 486-1229
- Pa & Ma's Horseback Riding (719) 486-3900
- Tabor Opera House Museum (719) 486-1147

AAA Pan Ark Lodge

AAA Pan Ark Lodge features spacious suites with natural, moss-rock fireplaces, modern, all-electric kitchens and beautiful mountain views. At the base of Mt. Elbert, these deluxe suites are designed for year-round gracious, comfortable vacations. A laundromat is available on-site for your convenience.

At the base of the highest mountains in Colorado, AAA Pan Ark Lodge is in the midst of a scenic paradise for hikers, photographers and fishing enthusiasts. Hike to the highest peaks in Colorado, play golf on the highest course in North America, raft the wild waters, visit historical ghost towns and mines. If you're an alpine or nordic skier, you're near Cooper, Copper Mountain, Vail and Beaver Creek ski resorts. Some of the nation's best cross-country skiing trails lie in the beautiful Twin Lakes/Independence Pass area.

Location: 9 miles south of Leadville on Highway 24, near milepost 187.

24 lodge suites with kitchenettes
Rates: $$$

Gene & Rosemarie Kulyan
5827 Highway 24 South (CB)
Leadville CO 80461
(719) 486-1063
(800) 443-1063

Pets: No
Elevation: 9,200
Credit Cards: VM
Open all year

Little Tundra Motel & Cottage

At an elevation of 10,065 feet, Little Tundra's motel units and cottage have a dramatic view of the 14,433-foot Mt. Elbert, the highest mountain in Colorado. Some units have kitchenettes, while all have cable television. Start your day off right with the furnished continental breakfast before heading out to a day of fun.

Little Tundra offers a discount pass to the local recreation complex that includes an Olympic-sized pool, a hot tub and weight room. You can fish in the Arkansas River from the premises or from other lakes nearby. In the winter, check out the many nearby ski resorts. Throughout the other seasons, take a hike or mountain bike through the beautiful mountain wildflowers.

Location: North of Leadville on Highway 91, near milepost 3.

1 housekeeping cottage
3 motel rooms with kitchenette
7 motel rooms without kitchenette
Rates: $$ to $$$

Larry & Oda Wilson
3164 N Highway 91 (CB)
Leadville CO 80461-9206
(719) 486-2783
(800) 779-2783

Pets: No
Elevation: 10,065
Credit Cards: VMD
Open all year

LIMON

Map: H-22

Limon, located on Colorado's high plains, is a convenient stopping point while traveling. Limon has a municipal swimming pool, nine-hole golf course and numerous picnic areas. Watch for the abundant wildlife on the plains surrounding Limon.

Fun Things to Do

- Pioneer Schoolhouse Museum (719) 775-2350
- Tamarack Golf Course (719) 775-9998
- Genoa Tower Museum (719) 763-2309

Limon KOA & Kamping Kabins™

These camper cabins are a convenient place to stop over on your way to Denver or Colorado Springs. Be sure to bring your own bedding and cooking equipment. The Limon KOA provides picnic tables, barbecue grills, clean restrooms, hot showers, a laundromat, a store, a playground for the kids and a heated swimming pool.

Location: Interstate 70, near Exit 361. Go to the Pizza Hut, then head two blocks north.

2 camper cabins
Camping available
Rates: $

Jim & Kay McCormick
Box 157 (CB)
Limon CO 80828-0157
(719) 775-2151

Pets: Yes
Elevation: 5,366
Credit Cards: VMD
Open March 15 to November 15

LOVELAND

Also see Estes Park. Map: C-16

Nestled at the base of the Big Thompson Canyon, Loveland offers access to a wide variety of recreation, cultural events and all the bustle of the big city — Denver is only 50 miles south. The Big Thompson Canyon provides easy entry to Estes Park and the spectacular Rocky Mountain National Park. Enjoy the easy pace in Loveland, where life moves a little slower and the people reflect values lost in many other places.

Fun Things to Do

- Benson Park Sculpture Garden (800) 258-1278
- Bronze Foundries (303)667-0991
- Little Thompson Valley Pioneer Museum (303) 532-2167
- Loveland Golf Course (303) 667-5256
- Loveland Museum & Gallery (303) 667-6070 or (303) 667-6130

River Court Lodge

Located 10 miles west of Loveland in the beautiful Big Thompson Canyon, the lodge has rooms with or without kitchenettes at reasonable rates. If you forgot anything at home, chances are the on-site store will have it. Relax and play in the outdoor heated pool or revel in the tranquillity of the area while sitting on the patio drinking your morning coffee. Loveland is the home of valentines and romance — there's even a charming gazebo by the river for weddings.

You can fish yards from your door on the Big Thompson River or, if you feel more adventurous, head to a nearby lake for water-skiing, swimming and sailing. Drive up the Big Thompson Canyon to Estes Park and Rocky Mountain National Park for hiking, backpacking and touring among dramatic mountain peaks. Discover the riding stables, Western rodeo, outdoor barbecues and wildlife of the area.

Location: Highway 34, near milepost 81.

1 housekeeping cabin
2 motel rooms with kitchenette
7 motel rooms without kitchenette
Rates: $$ to $$$

Terry & Carolyn Smith
1044 Big Thompson Canyon (CB)
Loveland CO 80537
(303) 667-3586
(800) 642-9272

Pets: No
Elevation: 6,200
Credit Cards: VMD
Open May 1 to September 15

MEEKER

Includes Trappers Lake. Map: E-5

Meeker, the gateway to the White River National Forest and the Flat Tops Wilderness, attracts many visitors year round who come for the excellent fishing and hunting. The White River National Forest has one of the largest elk herds in Colorado. There are 111 miles of fishable streams and 780 acres of lakes. In addition to hunting and fishing, you can enjoy boating, horseback riding, sightseeing, snowmobiling and cross-country skiing. Take advantage of the abundant four-wheel driving opportunities near Meeker — you can find almost every degree of difficulty somewhere in the area.

Fun Things to Do

- Dinosaur National Monument (303) 374-2216
- Meeker Golf Course (303) 878-5642
- White River Museum (303) 878-9982

Adams Lodge

This high-country hunting and fishing resort is located next to the White River National Forest in a gorgeous setting, snuggled against evergreens and aspens. The cabins range from one-room cabins to two-bedroom cabins with living rooms, tub baths and wood stoves. All cabins include dishes, utensils and linens.

There is also a ride-in fishing camp in the Flat Tops Wilderness Area at Marvine Lake, where you fish and your hosts cook and clean up. You can rent saddle horses, hire guides and put together a pack trip at the lodge. In the summer and fall months, enjoy the excellent hunting and fishing in the White River and Routt National Forests In the winter, you can rent a cabin for a cross-country ski trip in the Flat Tops Wilderness, or snowmobile around the many acres of National Forest.

Location: On County Road 8, east of Meeker, near milepost 29.

10 housekeeping cabins
Rates: $$$

Ron & Dona Hilkey
2400 County Rd. 12 (CB)
Meeker CO 81641
(303) 878-4312

Pets: Yes
Elevation: 7,600
Credit Cards: No
Open all year

Buford Hunting & Fishing Lodge & Store

On the Scenic Flat Tops Byway, these rustic and modern housekeeping cabins are adjunct to the beautiful White River in the center of the White River National Forest. Some of the cabins have fireplaces or wood stoves. The on-site grocery store provides sporting goods, gifts and gas.

There is excellent fishing and hunting in the White River National Forest — if you want, Buford Lodge can help set up drop camps and will provide guides. Chow down at the nearby restaurant, then rent a horse from the local stables to head on out into the wilderness.

Location: 22 miles east of Meeker on Trappers Lake Road (County Road 8) at Buford, near milepost 20.

11 housekeeping cabins
Rates: $$ to $$$

Harry Tucker
20474 County Rd. 8 (CB)
Meeker CO 81641
(303) 878-4745

Pets: Yes
Elevation: 7,000
Credit Cards: No
Open May 1 to November 15

Pollard's Ute Lodge

Enjoy high-mountain comfort at Pollard's Ute Lodge, located at the quiet end of the road up the White River Valley near the Scenic Flat Tops Byway. Prepare your favorite evening meal in a modern kitchen, then listen to the crackling fire while you relax and watch the stars. Or eat your meals outside on the picnic table under the deep blue sky.

The lodge is equipped with handicapped facilities.

Pollard's has unlicensed fishing opportunities on their private lake, or they can provide top-quality horses and drop camps. You can ride or hike through the Flat Tops wilderness area and the National Forest. Eat at the local restaurant while enjoying the scenery.

Location: 30 miles east of Meeker Highway County Road 8, near milepost 28.

6 housekeeping cabins
2 non-housekeeping cabins
Camping available
Rates: $$ to $$$$

Buck & Gloria Pollard
393 County Rd. 75 (CB)
Meeker CO 81641
(303) 878-4669

Pets: Yes
Elevation: 8,000
Credit Cards: No
Open May 15 to November 15

Rim Rock Cabins & Campground

The hosts like to "treat others as we like to be treated." Conveniently located on your route to Dinosaur National Monument, the cabins and campground is in a scenic Colorado setting. A store, laundromat and pool are located on the premises.

Reservations are required. You must stay a minimum of seven days.

Rim Rock is only a few miles from the town of Meeker, which has shopping and good restaurants. Fish for whitefish and trout in the White River, Lake Avery and Rio Blanco Lake. More than 80% of the county is on prime public land, so you can hike through miles and miles of State and National Forest areas. Hunt for deer, elk and antelope with rifle, bow, black powder or a camera.

Location: Highway 64, near milepost 73, only 3 miles west of Meeker.

2 housekeeping cabins
Camping available
Rates: $$

Wes & Linda DuBose
73179 Highway 64 (CB)
Meeker CO 81641
(303) 878-4486

Pets: Yes
Elevation: 6,250
Credit Cards: VMD
Open all year

Rustic Lodge & Saloon

Bring your own utensils and dishes to Rustic Lodge & Saloon, which offers a variety of kitchen-equipped housekeeping cabins, including towels, linens and televisions. All cabins sleep at least four people, and some have sitting rooms. Eat a hearty lunch and dinner at the lodge restaurant, then play pool or throw darts in the adjacent saloon. Soak in the hot tub while your children play in the spacious yard. There's also a laundromat for your convenience and a large, indoor meeting room for groups and family reunions.

Ask your host about their special packages for summer and hunting. Located at the east end of Meeker, the lodge is close to the National Forest lands for mountain biking, hiking and horseback riding. Fish the White River for whitefish and trout or hunt elk, deer and antelope.

Location: Highway 13, near milepost 42, at the east end of Meeker.

10 housekeeping cabins
Rates: $$

Harry Watt, owner
Melinda Parker, manager
173 1st St. (CB)
Meeker CO 81641
(303) 878-3136

Pets: No
Elevation: 6,380
Credit Cards: VM
Open all year

Sleepy Cat Guest Ranch

Located near Sleepy Cat Mountain in the scenic White River Valley, the Sleepy Cat Guest Ranch has modern rustic cabins with kitchens. When you don't want to cook, try the full-service restaurant and bar, featuring the finest steaks, prime rib, sea food and Rocky Mountain trout. The log lodge has a large fireplace and the walls are animated by many hunting and fishing trophies from near and far.

There is fishing all year in the White River, which flows through the ranch, plus in many lakes and streams nearby. Explore the surrounding mountains by horseback in the summer, or in the winter there is snowmobiling and cross-country skiing from your door with over 200 miles of marked trails.

Location: 18 miles east of Meeker on County Road 8, near milepost 16.

14 housekeeping cabins
6 motel rooms with kitchenette
Rates: $$

Clark, Charlotte, Steve & Debbie Wix
16064 County Rd. 8 (CB)
Meeker CO 81641
(303) 878-4413
(303) 878-5432

Pets: Yes
Elevation: 7,000
Credit Cards: VM
Open all year

Stagecoach Park

Along a ½-mile frontage on the scenic White River, you'll find two rustic housekeeping cabins on the 26-acre shaded grounds. Make sure you bring your own linens and utensils.

Fish right on the White River for whitefish and trout. There's also excellent hunting nearby, with large elk and mule deer herds. Close by, you'll find a golf course, riding stable and a swimming pool.

Location: 2 miles west of Meeker on Highway 13, near milepost 39.

3 housekeeping cabins
3 motel rooms with kitchenette
1 motel room without kitchenette
Camping available
Rates: $$ to $$$$$

Brady & Jill Kline
39084 Highway 13
P.O. Box 995 (CB)
Meeker CO 81641-0995
(303) 878-4334

Pets: Yes
Elevation: 6,000
Credit Cards: VM
Open all year

Two Rivers Guest Ranch

This is a special getaway, whether it's for hunting, fishing, backpacking or just enjoying solitude and back-country splendor. Located in one of the largest wilderness areas of the Rocky Mountains between the White River and Marvine Creek, the log cabins have fully equipped kitchenettes, linens, full baths and gas for cooking and heating. The rustic lodge has full-service facilities for dining and relaxing amid nature's finest country.

The ranch's specialty is back-country, horseback riding trips, either for hunting and fishing or for the spectacular scenery. The horses are experienced, gentle and sure-footed in the mountains. Ask your hosts about their full-service and drop-camp hunts — a special wilderness experience. Bring friends, bring the family, bring a business associate and by all means, bring a camera.

Location: Highway 8, near milepost 29.

5 housekeeping cabins
Camping available
Rates: $$$

Nigel & Sheryl Frazer
2633 County Road 12 (CB)
Meeker CO 81641-9211
(303) 878-4173

Pets: Yes
Elevation: 7,500
Credit Cards: No
Open May 15 to November 15

MESA VERDE AREA

Includes Mancos. Also see Dolores and Durango. Map: O-3

The Anasazi, or Ancient Ones, arrived in the Mancos Canyon area around 400 A.D. Today, Mesa Verde National Park preserves their history with several cliff dwellings and other ruins. By the end of the 1300s, the Anasazi were gone, forced from their canyon by severe drought and famine. You have a rare opportunity to visit the cliff dwellings and see how the Anasazi lived in this Four Corners region. The Mesa Verde area offers a wide range of historical tours and recreational activities, including horseback riding, fishing, hunting and hiking. Winter brings cross-country and downhill skiing as well as snowmobiling. Amid the breathtaking scenery, photographers and sightseers will delight in the ever-changing countryside.

Fun Things to Do

- Mesa Verde Mesa Verde National Park (303) 529-4465
- Mesa Verde Mesa Verde National Park Museum (303) 529-4475

SPRUCE TREE RUIN

A&A Mesa Verde RV Resort & Camper Cabins

This resort provides lodging next to Mesa Verde National Park. Bring your own bedding and cooking supplies. You can barbecue on the grill and eat at the picnic tables while watching your kids having fun in the playground. Swim laps in their new pool, then relax in the spa. For your convenience, the resort has clean showers, a laundromat and a store.

The resort stages country-western music shows for family entertainment. Horses, stabled 500 yards away, are available for horseback riding. Hike and bike in the National Park or spend your time among the famous ruins of the Indian cliff houses.

Location: Directly across from the entrance to Mesa Verde National Park.

2 camper cabins
Camping available
Rates: $

Abe & Alice Saunders
34979 Highway 160 (CB)
Mancos CO 81328
(303) 565-3517
(800) 972-6620

Pets: No
Elevation: 7,000
Credit Cards: VM
Open April 1 to November 1

Echo Basin Dude Ranch Resort & RV Park

Formerly a working ranch on more than 600 acres, Echo Basin is lush with meadows, streams and high timber forest areas. Stay either in deluxe A-Frame cabins with fireplaces or in the bunk house. You may gather your own firewood to throw on a campfire ring. The ranch has everything you need — a laundromat, a family-style restaurant and a country store.

Rent cabins by the night or the week, meals included.

In between the ranch-sponsored activities — horseback rides, hayrides and western cookouts — you can fish in the four stocked lakes or in the Mancos River, which runs through the ranch. Hunt in the fall, and rent snowmobiles or put on your cross-country skis during the winter. Spring and summer bring hiking and backpacking, tennis, volleyball, basketball and baseball. Be sure to see the many Southwest Colorado landmarks, including the Mesa Verde National Park, Durango CO mountains and the Southwestern desert.

Location: Three miles north of Highway 160, near milepost 59, on County Roads 44 and M.

18 non-housekeeping cabins
40 bunkhouse beds
Camping available
Rates: Call for prices

Mike & Karen Gray, Owners
Lee & Lorie Large, Managers
43747 Rd. M (CB)
Mancos CO 81328-9214
(303) 533-7800
(800) 426-1890

Pets: No
Elevation: 7,800
Credit Cards: VM
Open all year

Mesa Verde National Park see Mesa Verde Area. Also see Dolores and Durango. Map: O-3

MONTROSE

Map: K-5

Montrose has an abundance of things to do and see. Nearby Black Canyon National Monument is one of the most scenic and wild canyons in the world — the Gunnison River has slowly carved it to a depth of 2,200 feet. You can take raft trips through the canyon, allowing you to see otherwise-inaccessible areas. The Montrose area offers some of the best fishing in Colorado on the Gunnison, San Miguel and the Dolores Rivers. The Ridgway State Recreation Area provides boating, fishing, swimming and sunning opportunities. Visit the Ute Indian Museum, dedicated entirely to one tribe, to understand a bit of the region's history.

Fun Things to Do

- Black Canyon of the Gunnison National Monument (303) 249-7036
- Montrose Depot Museum (303) 249-2085
- Montrose Golf Course (303) 249-8551
- Orvis Hot Springs, Ridgway (303) 626-5324
- Ute Indian Museum (303) 249-3098

Montrose KOA & Kamping Kabins™

By bringing your own bedding and cooking equipment, these camper cabins at the Montrose KOA are an economical way to see this beautiful area of Colorado, including the Black Canyon of the Gunnison. A quiet country campground with in-town convenience, this is an ideal base camp for day trips to the canyon, the San Juan Mountains and Grand Mesa. The KOA also has a laundromat and a game room for those rare bad-weather days. They serve pancake breakfasts daily.

Check out the great fishing at nearby Ridgeway Recreation Area, Blue Mesa Reservoir, Morrow Point Dam and Crystal Reservoir. For the more adventurous, try river rafting and canoeing on the rivers nearby. If you're more inclined to stay dry, bike or hike the many miles of area trails.

Location: Highway 50, near milepost 94.

4 camper cabins
Camping available
Rates: $

Ken & LaVerne Rodda
200 North Cedar Ave. (CB)
Montrose CO 81401-5819
(303) 249-9177

Pets: Yes
Elevation: 5,700
Credit Cards: VM
Open April 15 to October 31

Nathrop: see Buena Vista. Map: J-12

Nederland: see Peak-to-Peak Scenic Highway Area. Map: E-14

New Castle: see Glenwood Springs. Map: F-7

OURAY

Map: M-6

As "The Little Switzerland of America," Ouray is an area of incomparable beauty nestled in the rugged San Juan Mountains. This scenic town is located on the Million Dollar Highway, named for the amount it cost to build in 1883. Ouray's Victorian architecture has been preserved and restored to recall the town's 19th century mining tradition. Take a leisurely walking tour of some of the distinctive homes and buildings. In the spring, summer and fall, rent a Jeep or take a guided tour to otherwise inaccessible areas with colorful names such as Yankee Boy Basin and Engineer Mountain. Another interesting adventure 13 miles west of Ouray is a tour of the Bachelor-Silver gold and silver mine, a working operation, where you'll be carried nearly 3,400 feet into the side of a Rocky Mountain peak. In the winter, you can enjoy snowmobiling, cross-country skiing and snowshoeing. Ouray remains true to the Western tradition of relaxed living and meaningful quality of life that many only dream about.

Fun Things to Do

Box Canyon Falls and Park (303) 325-4464
Chipeta Opry Show (303) 325-7354
Ouray County Historical Society & Museum (303) 325-4576
Ouray Hot Springs Pool (303) 325-4638

Ouray KOA & Kamping Kabins™

Visit the mountainous Ouray region from these camper cabins. Although you bring your own bedding and cooking utensils, your hosts serve delicious pancake breakfasts and Texas barbecue dinners. You'll share clean, ceramic tile restrooms, a hot tub and game room. By day, fish in the stocked trout pond; by night, watch a variety of entertaining movies at the campsite

The roads above Ouray were originally pack-train trails that were widened in time for wagons and stagecoaches. Ask your hosts about renting a four-wheel drive vehicle for exploring the high-country roads, or they'll give you a personally guided Jeep tour.

Location: Colorado Highway 23 off Highway 550, near milepost 98 (4 miles north of Ouray or 6 miles south of Ridgway).

6 camper cabins
Camping available
Rates: $

Dave Brunovsky
225 Highway 23
P.O. Box J (CB)
Ouray CO 81427-0534
(303) 325-4736

Pets: Yes
Elevation: 7,200
Credit Cards: VM
Open May 10 to October 1

PAGOSA SPRINGS AREA

Includes Chimney Rock. Map: F-9

Pagosa Springs is home to Wolf Creek Ski Area, which typically gets more snow than any other ski resort in Colorado. You can cross-country ski and snowmobile near Pagosa Springs as well. Explore the mystery of the Anasazi Indian ruins at nearby Chimney Rock or enjoy the hot springs, considered to be the hottest in the world. In fact, Pagosa Springs acquired its name from the Ute Indians who called the hot springs "Pagosah," or "healing waters." Fish in the many lakes, rivers and streams. Windsurf, waterski and sail on Navajo Lake, which extends southward 35 miles into New Mexico. Be sure to visit 100-foot Treasure Falls at the base of Wolf Creek Pass or just revel in the spectacular scenery.

Fun Things to Do

- Chimney Rock Indian Ruins (303) 264-2268
- Fairfield Pagosa Golf Course (719) 731-4141
- Fred Harman Art Museum (303) 731-5785
- Upper San Juan Historical Museum (303) 264-4424
- Wolf Creek Outfitters (303)264-5332

Bruce Spruce Ranch & Faris House Lodge

These clean, rustic log cabins, ideal for groups up to 30, have modern half-baths, kitchens with gas stoves, wood stoves for heat and centralized hot showers. They furnish all kitchen utensils and bed linens; you can use their washers and dryers as often as necessary. Throw out your fishing rod on a private fish pond (no license required).

This scenic ranch offers many activities, including horseback riding, and pack trips for fishing and hiking. The ranch, surrounded by thousands of acres of National Forest, is ideal for hunting deer, bear and elk. Close by, enjoy the four-wheel drive roads, Mesa Verde and other Indian ruins, narrow-gauge trains, hot mineral baths, wilderness hot springs and more.

Location: 16 miles northeast of Pagosa Springs on Highway 160, near milepost 158. Go ¼ mile northwest on the gravel road.

14 housekeeping cabins
5 lodge rooms
Camping available
Rates: $$

Craig & Eugenia Hinger
P.O. Box 296 (CB)
Pagosa Springs CO 81147-0296
(303) 264-5374
November to April: (806) 622-1346

Pets: Yes
Elevation: 8,200
Credit Cards: VM
Open May 20 to October 31

High Country Lodge & Cabins

High Country Lodge & Cabins are in the heart of Colorado's hunting, fishing, rafting and winter playground. Relax in their fully modern and furnished log cabins with fireplaces and fully equipped kitchens. All accommodations feature cable television, queen-sized beds and unlimited use of the two giant hot tubs and laundromat.

The resort is fully accessible for the disabled.

This resort offers super special ski packages for groups of 20 or more, which include lodging, lift tickets at the Wolf Creek Ski Area, two meals and use of hot tubs. After skiing, be sure to try the Ole Miner Steakhouse.

Location: 2½ miles east of Pagosa Springs on Wolf Creek Highway 160, near milepost 147.

4 housekeeping cabins
25 motel rooms without kitchenette
Rates: $$$$

Jim & James Watkins, Owners
Paul Bauer, Manager
P.O. Box 485 (CB)
Pagosa Springs CO 81147-0485
(303) 264-4181
(303) 264-2159

Pets: Yes
Elevation: 7,200
Credit Cards: VMAD
Open all year

Pagosa Riverside Camper Cabins & Campground

Bring your own bedding to these scenic, majestic mountain camper cabins on the banks of the San Juan River. They offer paddle boats on a private lake, a game room, a laundromat, a swimming pool and a store.

There is plenty of Colorado to see near the Pagosa Riverside Campground: It's only 60 miles to the famous Durango-Silverton Narrow Gauge Railroad, there's great fishing in the San Juan River, and you can indulge in nearby horseback rides, the Indian ruins at Chimney Rock, raft trips, tennis, hunting and hiking.

Location: 1½ miles east of Pagosa Springs on Highway 160, near milepost 146.

3 camper cabins
Camping available
Rates: $ to $$

Frank & Phyllis Tucker
P.O. Box 268 (CB)
Pagosa Springs CO 81147-0268
(303) 264-5874

Pets: Yes
Elevation: 7,000
Credit Cards: VM
Open May 1 to November 15

Piedra River Resort

These cozy, secluded log cabins with linens, dishes and cooking utensils are nestled among tall pines on the Piedra River, surrounded by the San Juan National Forest. The cowboy cookout area is a short horse ride up the trail, where you'll be served delicious food cooked outdoors.

You're bound to enjoy yourself, whether you fish, ride horses or just relax. The resort offers summer pack trips, plus hunting and outfitting. Your hosts, who have lived here since 1967, can point you to excellent hiking trails, fishing holes and other "inside" secrets of this Rocky Mountain region. Why not charter a fishing boat to catch Kokanee salmon and Northern pike — the resort owns a 20-foot cabin cruiser on Lake Navajo, 30 minutes away on the Colorado-New Mexico border.

Location: 20 miles west of Pagosa Springs and 35 miles east of Durango, on Highway 160, near milepost 121.

6 housekeeping cabins
4 non-housekeeping cabins
Rates: $$

David & Nancy Guilliams
P.O. Box 4190 (CB)
Pagosa Springs CO 81157-4190
(303) 731-4630

Pets: Yes
Elevation: 6,700
Credit Cards: VMD
Open April 15 to December 31

PAONIA

Includes Somerset. Also see Grand Mesa Area. Map: I-6

Paonia's name comes from peonies — the area was famed as having these wonderful spring wildflowers. Now is an agricultural center, it is known for apples, cherries and peaches. Paonia lies in the valley under the Grand Mesa, which has excellent and secluded fishing lakes and forests. As the midpoint of the West Elk Loop byway, Paonia is a quaint country town with restaurants, shops and curios. Nearby, Paonia State Park offers fishing, swimming, boating and camping.

Fun Things to Do

- Paonia North Fork Historical Society Museum (303) 527-4348
- Paonia State Park (303)921-5721

Crystal Meadows Ranch, Cabins & Campground

Nestled in a scenic river valley tucked between two mountain ranges, Crystal Meadows Ranch has accommodations varying from a two-bedroom log house with a full kitchen and a small bath, to a one-room log cabin with three beds and a shared bathroom. For your convenience, there is an on-site laundromat, a small grocery store, gas pumps and firewood. For conferences and reunions, they have both an outdoor pavilion and an indoor meeting room. A restaurant serves lunches and delectable dinners.

Fish in the privately stocked lake or in the gold-medal Anthracite Creek. Rent horses or hike in the nearby West Elk Mountains and the Raggeds, two vast and scenic wilderness areas. If you hunt, you'll find abundant deer and elk here.

Location: From Paonia, go 16 miles northeast on Highway 133. From Carbondale go southwest about 47 miles. Near milepost 24, go ½ mile on County Road 12 (Crested Butte-Kebler Pass Road).

1 camper cabin
2 housekeeping cabins
3 non-housekeeping rooms
Camping available
Rates: $$ to $$$$$

Bill & Kay Tennison
30682 County Rd. 12 (CB)
Somerset CO 81434-9625
(303) 929-5656

Pets: Yes
Elevation: 6,277
Credit Cards: No
Open Memorial Day to mid-November

Mariam's Bed & Breakfast

This quiet ranch setting, with the original buildings constructed in the late 1800s, offers bed and breakfast rooms surrounded by mountain splendor atop a 5,800-foot mesa. Streams running on each side of the house lull you to sleep at night. All rooms have shared baths. They serve bountiful breakfasts, with homemade breads and jams. Browse through the gift shop's unique works of art and crafts from Colorado. Mariam's has a cheerful, homey atmosphere for adults only.

Make advanced reservations for your hosts to pick you up at the North Fork Airport.

Area attractions include lake and stream fishing, four-wheel drive trails, hiking trails, hunting, skiing, antique and craft shops.

Location: 2 miles west and south of the village of Paonia on Stewart Mesa.

3 bed and breakfast rooms
Rates: $$$

Dorma & Mariam Eubank
1292-3950 Rd. (CB)
Paonia CO 81428
(303) 527-3613
(800)547-7096

Pets: No
Elevation: 5,800
Credit Cards: No
Open May 15 to November 15

Parlin: see Gunnison. Map: K-9

PEAK-TO-PEAK SCENIC HIGHWAY AREA

Includes Allenspark, Blackhawk, Central City, Eldora and Nederland.
Also see Boulder and Estes Park. Map F-14 to C-14.

This highway, which stretches along the Front Range from Central City to Estes Park, offers the highlights of Colorado mountain scenery, history and culture. Railroad buffs will want to drive up the grade of the Rollins Pass railroad, or seek out the route of the Switzerland Trail narrow-gauge to the small towns where Colorado's first gold strikes were made. The Central City and Blackhawk mining area boomed during the late 19th century; its gold helped build the mansions of Denver as well as its own glamorous historic hotels and saloons. Recently, many of the old hotels and saloons have been restored as limited-stakes gambling casinos, while the Central City Opera House is well known for its international-quality opera productions during the summer. To the north, you'll pass through Nederland and Eldora, old goldmining towns that produced tungsten through the 1940s. Longs Peak presents its most dramatic face to the highway as you climb a pass and descend to Estes Park.

Fun Things to Do

- Central City Opera House, Central City (303) 582-5202
- Gilpin County Historical Society & Museum, Central City (303) 582-5283
- Lace House Museum, Blackhawk (303) 582-5382
- Nederland Historical Society & Museum, Nederland (303) 258-3575
- Teller House Museum, Central City (303) 279-8306 or (303) 582-3200

Allenspark Lodge

This classic, high-mountain bed and breakfast lodge is nestled among the flower-starred village. The three-story, hand-hewn log lodge, constructed of native stone and Ponderosa Pine, offers the time and place to create sweet memories to last a lifetime. Many of the comfortable, private rooms have private baths with a shower or a big tub. The other rooms, all homey and each different (some with sinks, some not) have access to a large, private shower. All rooms have mountain views and are furnished with original handmade pine furniture from the 1930s. Your hosts offer warm hospitality to create a special magic to make your stay unforgettable. Relax your muscles in a private hot tub or enjoy the quiet game room and eclectic library. The Allenspark Lodge serves delicious continental breakfasts and lunches along with wine and imported beer.

In beautiful Estes Park, rent four-wheel drive vehicles or horses, or spend the day making an assault on Longs Peak — the magnificent surroundings include miles of incomparable views.

Location: Off of Route 7 in Allenspark, near milepost 15.

3 housekeeping cabins
13 bed and breakfast rooms
Rates: $$$$

Mike & Becky Osmun
P.O. Box 247 (CB)
Allenspark CO 80510-0247
(303) 747-2552

Pets: No
Elevation: 8,500
Credit Cards: VM
Open all year

Arapaho Ranch Cabins

Arapaho Ranch is nicely situated in a valley between Nederland and Eldora, on the Middle Boulder Creek. The cabins are ½-mile inside the gate away from the highway. Most are along the stream, others are close by with a panoramic view. With roofed porches and rustic charm, each cabin has two to four bedrooms with double beds and plenty of blankets and pillows, gas heat, a bathroom, refrigerator, stove and equipment for light housekeeping. Bring or rent sheets, pillowcases and towels. Your kids will enjoy the playground, while groups can indulge in activities in the new recreation hall.

Be on the lookout for deer, raccoons or beavers that may meander through the ranch. And there's always a Monday night cookout. As a fishing enthusiast, you'll have exclusive fishing rights to Middle Boulder Creek, but you can also hike or drive to the many high mountain lakes. While backpacking up to the Continental Divide, notice the many beautiful and unfrequented pine dells, meadows and scenic points. If you're in the mood for gambling, this ranch is within an easy drive to Central City.

Location: 17 miles west of Boulder on Highway 119, near milepost 25. Turn off on Eldora Road (County Road 130). Go 1 mile to the gate.

10 housekeeping cabins
Rates: $$$

Kayla Evans & Maryanne Flynn

1250 Eldora Rd. (CB)
Nederland CO 80466-9525
Pets: Yes
Elevation: 8,200
Credit Cards: No
Open May 1 to October 1

Dory Hill KOA & Kamping Kabins™

Clean and friendly, the Dory Hill KOA has eight camper cabins conveniently located near Central City and Denver. The campground has a heated swimming pool, game room, playground, laundromat, gasoline, propane and video rentals.

Although they're the nearest mountain camper cabins to Denver and the Rocky Mountains, they're also near to historic Central City and Blackhawk, with their museums, opera house and casinos, Buffalo Bill's grave, the Coors Brewery, fishing and ghost towns.

Location: From I-70, take U.S. 6 to Highway 119 north of Blackhawk 5 miles to Route 46, near milepost 12. ½. Go east ½ mile on Route 46.

8 camper cabins
Camping available
Rates: $ to $$

Norman & Kathy Condreay
661 Highway 46 (CB)
Golden CO 80403
(303) 582-9979

Pets: Yes
Elevation: 9,230
Credit Cards: VMD
Open all year

Goldminer Hotel

This 1897 Hotel is the centerpiece of the Eldora National Historic District. Check into one of the fully modernized, yet Gold-Rush style rooms or suites, some with private bathrooms. The "Rocky Ledge" cabin sleeps six and has a kitchen, fireplace and an old-fashioned bathtub. Rooms also include a delicious breakfast to start your day right. At night, soak your road-weary muscles in the communal hot tub.

Depending on the seasons, you can take back-country jeep, cross-country ski, snow cat and horseback tours. Ride their free shuttle to the casinos of Central City. The Goldminer is adjacent to the Indian Peaks Wilderness, where you can hike to the Continental Divide. And the quaint town of Boulder is only 30 minutes away.

Location: Off of Highway 119, near milepost 25.

1 housekeeping cabin
5 historic hotel rooms
Rates: $$ to $$$$$
Carol Rinderknecht & Scott Bruntjen
601 Klondyke Ave. (CB)
Eldora CO 80466-9542
Information: (303) 258-7770
Reservations: (800) 422-4629

Pets: Yes
Elevation: 8,600
Credit Cards: VM
Open all year

Pikes Peak: see Colorado Springs Area, Cripple Creek, Divide and Lake George. Map: I-15 to I-17

Platoro: see Antonito. Map: O-11

Poncha Springs: see Salida. Map: J-13

POUDRE RIVER CANYON AREA

Includes Bellvue. Also see Red Feather Lakes. Map: B:14

Poudre Canyon, also known as Cache la Poudre, enjoys a colorful past. Even the name has a history — in 1840, French freighters camped at the mouth of the canyon west of Fort Collins. A heavy snow fell, forcing them to reduce their load, so they buried their gun powder, or "cache la poudre," right there. In 1879, settlers built a rough road over the cache, which soon led to a steady stream of cabins. Today, the canyon is home to a wide range of resorts and recreation activities. Designated Colorado's first National Wild and Scenic River in 1986, the Cache la Poudre River flows through the Roosevelt National Forest. Tourists are drawn to this area's rugged beauty, the friendly people and easy way of life.

Fun Things to Do

- Avery House (303) 221-0533
- City Park Nine Golf Course (303) 221-6650
- Collindale Golf Course (303) 221-6651
- Fort Collins Museum (303) 221-6738
- Glen Echo General Store, Gift Shop and Restaurant (800) 881-2208, (303)881-2208
- Link-N-Greens (303) 221-4818
- Ptarmigan Golf Course (303) 226-6600
- Southridge Golf Course (303) 226-2828

Glen Echo Resort

In the heart of Roosevelt National Forest, Glen Echo Resort is on the Poudre River, Colorado's "Trout Route." Choose between modern cottages with full kitchens and baths, rustic cabins with kitchens and shared bathroom-shower facilities or family mountain homes with large living rooms and everything but food. Several of the cabins have decks overlooking the Poudre River. All cottages have dishes, cooking supplies, bedding and linens. There is a laundromat, a casual restaurant with good home cooking and a general store carrying groceries, souvenirs and the largest selection of authentic Native American jewelry and crafts in northern Colorado. While there, check out the North American and African wildlife exhibit.

Enjoy fishing on Colorado's only designated wild and scenic river, right out your cabin door. It's a short drive to Red Feather Lakes for more fishing, or you can hike around Comanche Peak Wilderness in the Mummy Range.

Location: 41 miles west of Fort Collins on Highway 14, near milepost 90½.

17 housekeeping cottages and cabins
Camping available
Rates: $$ to $$$$

Sam Shoultz & Ken Matzner
31503 Poudre Canyon Dr. (CB)
Bellvue CO 80512-9312
(303) 881-2208
(800) 348-2208

Pets: Yes
Elevation: 7,200
Credit Cards: VM
Open May 1 to November 1

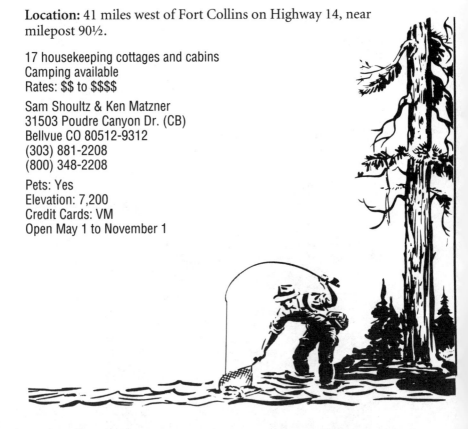

Poudre River Resort

These modern cabins, adjacent to the beautiful Poudre River, high in the Rocky Mountains, have ample bedrooms with linens, bathrooms with showers and towels and fully equipped kitchens with electric or gas ranges. For relaxation, you have the option of soaking in the community hot tub or curling up by the fireplace with a favorite movie you rented from the on-site video service. For added convenience, there's a grocery store, a snack bar and a laundromat.

You'll find excellent hiking trails and stocked fishing lakes, both at the resort and in the nearby mountains. If you get tired of cabin cooking, dine at one of the local restaurants.

Location: 45 miles northwest of Fort Collins, on Highway 14, near milepost 89.

10 housekeeping cabins
Camping available
Rates: $$$

Don & Donna Moberly
33021 Poudre Canyon Dr. CB)
Bellvue CO 80512-9426
(303) 881-2139

Pets: Yes (one dog on leash at all times)
Elevation: 7,200
Credit Cards: VM
Open all year

Spencer Heights Resort

Rocks and trees populate this wonderful resort on 1,100 feet of Poudre River frontage. You can rent either modern or rustic cabins, some with fireplaces or wood stoves. After a day spent fishing or skiing in the backcountry, what better way to end the day than dining at the fine restaurant, then soaking in the hot tub and stretching out by the fire!

In spring and summer months, you'll enjoy top-notch fishing in the wild and scenic Poudre River, while in the winter, go cross-country skiing on nearby trails. The scenery is gorgeous any time of the year.

Location: 52 miles west of Fort Collins on Highway 14, near milepost 78.

9 housekeeping cabins
3 non-housekeeping cabins
Rates: Call for prices

David Durst & Betty Van Amburg
44595 Poudre Canyon (CB)
Bellvue CO 80512
(303) 881-2172

Pets: Yes
Elevation: 8,200
Credit Cards: No
Open all year

Sportsman's Lodge

Since 1931, Sportsman's Lodge has been a place for guests to gather and relax, plus it provides fun fishing, hunting and hiking experiences — it's great for family reunions! The lodge's beautiful setting and modest furnishings, many from the '30s, make you think time has stood still. The rustic housekeeping cabins are clean and charming, featuring woodburning stoves "just like Grandma cooked on." Modern bathrooms and showers are in separate buildings. One cabin has a kitchen, sleeping room and a bathroom with a shower. For your convenience, a small store sells groceries, fishing licenses and tackle.

The Sportsman's Lodge is in a beautiful location in the canyon on the river, within minutes of Poudre Falls, Chambers Lake and Cameron Pass. In the spring and summer, take advantage of river and lake fishing, hiking, rafting, horseback riding, mountain biking and quiet relaxation. You'll have ample opportunities to photograph the abundant wildlife, including moose, bighorn sheep and birds (especially the hummingbirds). Fall brings a color tour of turning aspens and big game hunting. Winter provides the backdrop for cross-country skiing, snowmobiling and ice fishing.

Location: 54 miles west of Fort Collins on Highway 14, near milepost 79.

12 housekeeping cabins
RV camping available
Rates: $$

John & Lee Ann Schenk
44174 Poudre Canyon Highway (CB)
Bellvue CO 80512-9604
(303) 881-2272

Pets: Yes
Elevation: 7,780
Credit Cards: No
Open all year

Pueblo: see Rye and Cañon City.

Rand: see Gould.

RED FEATHER LAKES

Also see Poudre River Canyon Area. Map: B-14

Red Feather Lakes, a group of 14 lakes, are about 50 miles northwest of Fort Collins. Six of the lakes are open to public recreation, especially for trout fishing and boating. The scenic beauty of the San Isabel and Roosevelt National Forests boasts abundant wildflowers and wildlife: look for elk, antelope, mule deer, bears, quail, grouse, mountain lions, Big Horn sheep and wild turkey. Wintertime brings cross-country skiers, snowmobilers, snowshoers and ice-fishing enthusiasts to the area.

Fun Things to Do

- Beaver Meadows Restaurant, Lounge and Cross Country Skiing (800) 462-5870
- Red Feather Lakes Village (800) 462-5870
- Roosevelt National Forest (303) 498-1375

Alpine Lodge

These cabins are located near the Roosevelt National Forest. There is a small gift shop on the premises. Two of the cabins are modern and have kitchens and bathrooms; one sleeps 5-6 people and the other sleeps 3. The third cabin is rustic — it has a kitchen but no bathroom and only has cold running water; it sleeps 2. There is also a two-bedroom mobile home available for rent that sleeps 6. In all of the cabins all you need to bring is groceries — all other supplies are provided.

There is a golf course nearby (sand greens), and fishing in six public Red Feather Lakes and in nearby streams. Head out on the hiking trails, rent a horse for riding in the forest, and go snowmobiling and cross-country skiing in the winter. Come and enjoy the scenic and unspoiled beauty of the Colorado Rockies!

Location: 45 miles northwest of Fort Collins, about 26 miles west of Highway 287, south ½-mile from Red Feather Lakes Village.

3 housekeeping cabins
1 trailer for rent
Rates: $$

Emma, Lowell & Tammy Grauberger
P.O. Box 180 (CB)
Red Feather Lakes CO 80545-0180
(303) 881-2933

Pets: No
Elevation: 8,363
Credit Cards: No
Open all year

Beaver Meadows Resort

In a high mountain wooded area, Beaver Meadows Resort adjoins National Forest land, bringing you comfortable accommodations to suit your style — from modern cabins complete with fireplaces and full kitchens to luxurious condominiums. Choose a unit close to the restaurant and lounge or a secluded cabin overlooking the North Fork of the Poudre River. Either way, relax in the community sauna after a tough day of activities. If you're planning a conference, the resort offers large meeting rooms or, if you're planning your honeymoon, get married in the on-site wedding facilities.

Fish in the private ponds during the summer and skate on them in the winter. Other nearby winter activities include cross-country skiing on groomed trails, past pine and spruce trees with boughs drooping under the weight of snow. If you need them, the resort provides skiing lessons. Spring brings melting streams, budding aspen and tiny flowers snuggled in the new grass. Summer means songbirds, wildflowers, fresh-washed air after a summer shower and night stars undimmed by city lights. Autumn explodes with color in golden aspen, deep blue skies and the heavy green of the pines.

Location: 50 miles northwest of Fort Collins, 6 miles northwest of Red Feather Lakes on the North Fork of the Poudre River.

5 housekeeping cabins
Camping available
Rates: $$ to $$$$

Don, Diane & Linda Weixelman
P.O. Box 178 (CB)
Red Feather Lakes CO 80545-0178
(800) 462-5870

Pets: No
Elevation: 8,300
Credit Cards: VM
Open all year

Trout Lodge

Get your fishing rods ready — this lodge wasn't named for nothing! Set in a scenic, quiet atmosphere, these all-modern, completely furnished log cabins feature comfortable rooms with fireplaces. There is a central meeting room to accommodate larger groups and a sports court for family games.

You'll enjoy trout fishing in any of the five state lakes and the three streams nearby. Hiking trails in the local forests and mountains are unequaled — the meadows of wildflowers and abundant wildlife are a photographer's heaven. And don't forget to bring your skis, snowshoes and ice-fishing pole in the winter.

Location: Take 287 north to Livermore, then turn west to Red Feather Lakes. At the Post Office, turn right to Lake Ramona.

6 housekeeping cabins
Rates: $$ to $$$

Steven & Charlotte Schliening
1078 Ramona Dr.
P.O. Box 126 (CB)
Red Feather Lakes CO 80545-0126
(303) 881-2964

Pets: Yes
Elevation: 8,600
Credit Cards: VMA
Open all year

REDSTONE-MARBLE AREA

Includes Redstone and Marble. Also see Carbondale. Map: H-8

The Redstone-Marble area is a historic mining area with ghost towns and dramatic mountain scenery. Redstone was founded by John Cleveland Osgood at the turn of the century as a model community to house employees of his coal mines. Although the workers and their families were housed in simple cabins, Osgood built the luxurious Cleveholm Castle for himself, furnished with Tiffany chandeliers and Italian paintings. Marble was best known for its quarries, which produced a pure marble that rivaled Italy's Carrerra marble. Some of it was used in the Lincoln Memorial monument and the Tomb of the Unknown Soldier. The difficulties of mountain transportation closed down the quarries, but you can still reach them by four-wheel drive vehicles.

Fun Things to Do

* Marble Historical Society & Museum (303) 963-2143 or (303) 963-3035
* Redstone Castle Cleveholm Museum (303) 963-3463
* Redstone Historical Museum (303) 963-1025

Avalanche Ranch

Avalanche Ranch offers 45 acres of lush countryside overlooking the Crystal River and the Elk Mountain Range and surrounded by the White River National Forest. The original 1913 farmhouse, featured in several national publications, has been restored to a country bed and breakfast inn, romantically decorated with antiques. Its restaurant serves breakfast to cabin guests; all other meals by private arrangement The cozy log cabins, offering abundant views, have full kitchens, sleeping lofts, porches, private yards, picnic tables and barbecues. The ranch is an excellent place for children — they can play in tree house or the kid's cabin, outfitted with games and toys.

Smoking is not permitted in the ranch buildings.

Avalanche Ranch provides an ideal setting for romantic getaways, family reunions and weddings. Explore the trails that skirt the valley on foot, by mountain bike, on horseback, on snoeshoes or on cross-country skis. The historic towns of Redstone and Marble Quarry are nearby, while five major downhill ski resorts, including Aspen/Snowmass, are within an hour's drive. The famous Glenwood Springs Hot Springs pool is just 25 minutes away. Local trout fishing is world-renowned in the Crystal, Roaring Fork and Frying Pan Rivers.

Location: Highway 133, near milepost 56.

11 housekeeping cabins
4 bed and breakfast rooms
Rates: $$$$$

Jim & Sharon Mollica
12863 Highway 133 (CB)
Redstone CO 81623
(303) 963-2846

Pets: Yes
Elevation: 7,000
Credit Cards: VMD
Open all year

Chair Mountain Ranch

At the base of Chair Mountain, nestled among the trees along the Crystal River, this ranch is a peaceful mountain retreat, with fully equipped, two bedroom housekeeping cabins.

You can fish for gold-medal trout on ranch grounds from the Crystal River, bathe in medicinal hot springs along the river or visit historic Redstone with its quaint shops. Add a little excitement by whitewater rafting on the Roaring Fork or Colorado Rivers. Check out the local riding stables for breakfast rides to several-day pack trips. Your hosts can arrange horse or four-wheel drive vehicles to get to excellent deer and elk hunting in the area. Hike or bike on the abundant, scenic trails — you can rent mountain bikes in Redstone. As your hosts say, "You won't need a vacation to recover from your vacation when you spend it at Chair Mountain Ranch."

Location: Highway 133, near milepost 46.

5 housekeeping cabins
3 camper cabins
Rates: $$ to $$$$$

Jim & Cathy Clark
0178 County Rd. 3 (CB)
Redstone CO 81623
(303) 963-9522

Pets: Yes
Elevation: 7,640
Credit Cards: VM
Open all year, weather permitting

Prospect Mountain Ranch

On a 100-acre meadow surrounded by 13,000-foot peaks, Prospect Mountain Ranch is a working horse ranch with rustic housekeeping cabins situated on the Crystal River. Cast your fishing rod in one of the two trout ponds or ride horses with the cowboys here.

See the local sights while hiking or mountain biking, or take a four-wheel drive road to Marble Quarry and Old Crystal Mill. The ranch is also close to Redstone Castle, Glenwood Hot Springs and Aspen.

Location: Highway 133, near milepost 46.

10 housekeeping cabins
1 trailer
Camping available
Rates: Call for prices

John & Theresa Armstrong
P.O. Box 1163 (CB)
Marble CO 81623-1163
Summer: (303) 963-2323
Off-season: (303) 925-1994

Pets: No
Elevation: 7,700
Credit Cards: No
Open May 2 to October 1

Rico: see Dolores. Map: N-4

Rocky Mountain National Park: see Estes Park, Map: C-14, Grand Lake, Map: D-13, Loveland, Map: C-16, Peak-to-Peak Scenic Highway Area, Map: F-14 and Winter Park, Map: E-14

Royal Gorge: see Cañon City, Map: K-19, Coaldale, Map: K-14, Howard, Map: K-13 and Salida, Map: J-13

RYE

Although considered a cattle ranching region, Rye is close to a number of forests and lakes. Lake Isabel in the San Isabel National Forest offers aquatic activity from fishing to paddle boating. Hike, bike or ride horses through the many trails — you'll see a variety of birds and wildflowers during the spring and summer and spectacular fall colors in autumn. In the winter, bring your cross-country skis and make tracks throughout the forest. Golf courses and museums can be found in nearby Pueblo.

Fun Things to Do

- Bishop Castle (719) 564-4366
- El Pueblo Museum (719) 554-5274
- Paws Children's Museum, Pueblo (719) 543-0130
- Pueblo City Park Golf Course (719) 561-4946
- Pueblo West Golf Course (719) 547-2280
- Robbers Roost Western Museum (719) 489-3559
- Walking Stick Golf Course, Pueblo (719) 584-3400

Aspen Acres Cabins & RV Park

Vacation in the majestic, quiet mountains of the San Isabel National Forest. Aspen Acres, as the name suggests, is situated amid thousands of acres of aspen and pine trees. Bring your own bedding and cooking utensils when staying in these economical camper cabins. For your convenience, the RV park has clean restrooms and a laundromat.

Aspen Acres is 2 miles north of Lake Isabel, so be prepared to fish for hours on end. Check out the area's hiking and cross-country skiing trails. And don't miss hunting opportunities amid the incredible fall colors.

Location: 25 miles south of Pueblo on I-25, take exit 74, head west on Highway 165; near milepost 16½.

6 camper cabins
Camping available
Rates: $

Al & Rita Jirsa
HCR. 75
P.O. Box 149 (CB)
Rye CO 81069-0149
(719) 485-3275

Pets: Yes
Elevation: 8,700
Credit Cards: No
Open all year

Colorado Ranch Connection, Inc.

A real working ranch near the Greenhorn Mountains in the Sangre de Cristo Range, the Christenson Ranch has 2,400 acres of private land near San Isabel National Forest. Ranch terrain stretches from irrigated hay meadows to deep sandstone canyons and pine and spruce forests. Anyone who loves horses and the ranch way of life will love vacationing here! You'll enjoy delicious, family style home-cooked meals at the main ranch house or meals cooked cowboy style over an open fire. You can stay at the ranch guest house or in a housekeeping cabin.

Reservations are required since accommodations are limited to eight guests per week. Prices includes all meals. You may bring your own horse — they provide suitable feed and safe corrals.

On your horse, you'll check pastures for sick cattle, move cattle from one pasture to another, or just peacefully explore the ranch and the surrounding area. Take a "wildlife safari," fish in nearby streams and lakes, or hike and backpack in the Greenhorn Mountains.

Location: Take I-25 to Exit 74 to Highway 165 west. Turn right on Old San Isabel Road. The ranch is 4 miles northwest of Rye.

1 housekeeping cabin
2 bed and breakfast rooms in ranch guest house
Rates: $$$$ to $$$$$

Roy & Shannon Christenson
8464 Old San Isabel Rd. (CB)
Rye CO 81069
(719) 489-2266

Pets: No
Elevation: 7,000
Credit Cards: No
Open all year

J. J.'s Cabins, General Store & RV Park

Bring your own cooking utensils and dishes to these two cabins overlooking Lake Isabel. One cabin sleeps four and has a kitchenette; the other sleeps six and has no kitchen facilities. You'll get bed and bath linens when you arrive. Barbecue your freshly caught trout on the outdoor barbecue grills and enjoy the view while eating at the picnic tables. The kids will have fun in the video game arcade while you shop for fishing licenses and gear, groceries and gifts in the general store.

Reservations are suggested.

Rent row boats and paddle boats to glide over the lake or go hiking and birdwatching in the surrounding areas.

Location: Off of Highway 165, near milepost 19.

1 housekeeping cabin
1 non-housekeeping cabin
Camping available
Rates: $$$

Jerry & Coco Duran
Westmore Star Rt.
P.O. Box 115 (CB)
Rye CO 81069-0115
(719) 489-2601
October 15 to April 25: (714) 974-6865

Pets: Yes
Elevation: 8,600
Credit Cards: VM
Open May 1 to October 15

The Lodge at San Isabel

These cabins, located in the mountains next to the trout-stocked Lake San Isabel, are ideal for groups and family reunions; each room sleeps up to eight people. Bring your own dishes and cooking utensils — the lodge provides towels and linens. Some have fireplaces and kitchens. There's a cafe, grocery store, service station and gift shop full of curios.

Ask your hosts about river rafting and snowmobile tours. Rent rowboats and paddle boats or go horseback riding, hiking, motorcycling and mountain biking or head off to explore the old gold mines.

Location: 10 miles north of Rye on Highway 165, near milepost 19.

8 housekeeping cabins
6 non-housekeeping cabins
Rates: $$ to $$$

Dave & Shirley Harmon
HCR 75, Box 123 (CB)
Rye CO 81069-0231
(719) 489-2280

Pets: Yes
Elevation: 8,700
Credit Cards: VM
Open all year

SALIDA

Enjoy a myriad of recreational activities in this historical area. In the spring, cross-country ski until late April when the fishing gets good. During the summer, mountain bike, hike and raft the wild waters to your heart's content. Or, if you prefer, explore the many ghost towns on four-wheel drive roads. When the fall colors change, you can photograph the majestic scenery or take part in some of the best big game hunting in the state. In any season, take a dip in the Hot Springs swimming pool, one of the finest indoor warm-water pools.

Fun Things to Do

- Arkansas Valley Expeditions (800) 833-RAFT
- Fun Time Jeep Tours (719) 539-2962
- Moondance River Expeditions, Ltd. (719) 539-2113
- River Runners Ltd. Colorado: (800) 332-9100;
  out of state: (800) 525-2081
- Salida Golf Course (719) 539-6373
- Salida Hot Springs (719) 539-6738
- Salida Museum (719) 539-4804
- The Powerhouse Players, June to August: (719) 539-2455;
  September to May: (214) 941-1489

Log Cabin Court

These clean, modern 50-year-old cabins, situated in a picturesque and peaceful place on the bank of the Arkansas River, all have kitchens, private bathrooms, cable television and maid service. You'll sleep comfortably on extra-long double beds.

There's lots to do here by the Arkansas River State Recreation Area. Ask your host for suggestions and tour information.

Location: Off of Highway 291, near milepost 8.

2 housekeeping cabins
Rates: $$

Robert Barnes
536 E. First
P.O. Box 1071(CB)
Salida CO 81201-1071
(719) 539-4793

Pets: Yes
Elevation: 7,036
Credit Cards: No
Open all year

Wagon Wheel Guest Ranch

Experience real old-fashioned Western hospitality, friendliness and a laid-back way of life at Wagon Wheel Guest Ranch. Located along the South Arkansas River and surrounded by the Sawatch Mountain Range, these log cabins are completely furnished with fully equipped kitchenettes and shower-baths. There are no televisions or phones in the cabins to disturb you. Fish in the privately stocked trout pond on the property, then cook your catch on the barbecue grills and eat your meal on the shady picnic tables in this mountain paradise.

Your hosts can arrange four-wheel drive tours and raft trips or you can choose your own activity: exploring nearby ghost towns, photographing the wildflowers and wildlife, hiking, fishing, swimming, golfing, horseback riding and gondola rides.

Location: 11 mile west of Salida, off of Highway 50, near milepost 211.

6 housekeeping cabins
Rates: $$$ to $$$$

Bill & Frankie Sustrich
16760 County Rd. 220 (CB)
Salida CO 81201-9428
(719) 539-6063

Pets: Yes (attended only)
Elevation: 8,200
Credit Cards: No
Open May 1 to September 30

San Isabel: see Rye. Map: M-17
Sargents: see Gunnison. Map: K-9

SILVERTON

Map: M-6

Step back in history and stay awhile in Silverton. For years, this area has produced gold, silver and other metals. Today, Old Town Square invites you to browse shops filled with Old West charm and rare antiques. Visit the Grand Imperial Hotel, built in 1882 — a perfect example of Victorian architecture. Because of the atmosphere, several Western movies have been filmed here, not only to take advantage of the historic look, but to capture the splendorous mountain magic as well. The area is filled with Jeep trails, so bring your four-wheel drive vehicle or rent a Jeep. For a truly memorable vacation, ride the Durango-Silverton Narrow Gauge Railroad starting in Durango, then spend some time in Silverton reliving history.

Fun Things to Do

* Durango-Silverton Narrow Gauge Railroad (303) 247-2733
* San Juan County Historical Society Museum (303) 387-5830
* Silverton Lakes Jeep Rental (303) 387-5721

Molas Lake Park, Camper Cabins & Campground

On the banks of trout-stocked Molas Lake, the most spectacular view in all of Colorado makes staying in these "tent cabins" or the 22-foot tepee worthwhile. Bring your own bedding and cooking gear to this excellent, economical place to stay while reveling in the San Juan Mountains' scenery. The country store carries groceries, fishing licenses, wood and sandwiches. There's also a recreation room, hot showers and a laundromat for your convenience.

Molas Lake sponsors breakfast horseback and steak cookout rides, offers fish cleaning services and rents canoes and provides other entertainment. The area abounds with hiking and four-wheel drive trails in the San Juan Mountains, gold panning and ghost towns. Molas Lake is truly the "land of happy campers."

Location: 5 miles south of Silverton on Highway 550, near milepost 66.

3 camper cabins
Camping available
Rates: $

Shelia Baker & Robert Haisler
P.O. Box 776 (CB)
Silverton CO 81433-0776
(303) 387-5410

Pets: Yes
Elevation: 10,500
Credit Cards: No
Open May 25 to October 1

St. Paul Cross-Country Ski & Summer Lodge

This 10-year-old lodge offers packaged cross-country ski vacations in the San Juan Mountains. Genuinely rustic, with kerosene lamps and wood stoves, these rooms provides comfort in the style of the 1890s, yet have indoor plumbing and a communal sauna. Choose your option: a cozy housekeeping cabin, a lodge room or an economical dormitory room. They serve catered meals family style in between skiing.

Location: Off of Highway 550, near milepost 80.

1 housekeeping cabin
5 lodge rooms
8 dormitory rooms
Rates: Call for prices

Chris & Donna George
1647 Greene St
P.O. Box 463 (CB)
Silverton CO 81433-0463
(303) 387-5494
(303) 387-5367

Pets: No
Elevation: 11,440
Credit Cards: No
Open all year

Somerset: see Paonia. Map: I-7

SOUTH FORK

Includes Wagon Wheel Gap. Map: N-10

South Fork is situated at the edge the San Luis Valley, one of the biggest intermountain valleys in the world. It's a convenient hub to a variety of nearby recreation activities: Wolf Creek Ski Area, fishing, hiking and sightseeing in the beautiful scenery.

Fun Things to Do

- Blue Creek Restaurant (800) 326-6408, (719) 658-2479
- Chinook Smokehouse (800) 238-6837, (719) 873-9993
- River's Edge Trophy Trout Fishing (719) 873-5993

Aspen Ridge Cabins & RV Park

The clean, modern cabins at Aspen Ridge, "where the quiet is beautiful," have kitchenettes, fireplaces or wood stoves and cable television. They furnish all linens, pots and pans. There is a laundromat, shower facilities and a recreation hall for groups.

Nearby, the Rio Grand River boasts excellent gold-medal trout fishing or, if you prefer, your hosts can supply you with a map to the many local lakes. Hike into the unusual Wheeler Geologic Area, a landscape of pinnacles, canyons and arches accessible only by foot. Make Aspen Ridge your cabin and fishing headquarters in Southern Colorado.

Location: Off of Highway 149, near milepost 1, ½ mile northwest of the junction at Highway 160.

7 housekeeping cabins
Camping available
Rates: $$

Charles & Brenda Murray
0710 Highway 149 West (CB)
South Fork CO 81154
(719) 873-5921

Pets: Yes
Elevation: 8,250
Credit Cards: VM
Open all year

Blue Creek Lodge, Cabins, Campground & Restaurant

This is a vacationers paradise — a haven for fishing enthusiasts, hunters, skiers, hikers and photographers. The lodge offers hospitality, home-cooked meals, modern housekeeping cabins or lodge rooms with a private bath. Relax at the soda fountain and stock up on curios from the gift shop.

In the winter, try tubing, ice skating, snowmobiling, cross-country or alpine skiing at the Wolf Creek Ski Area. In the spring and summer months, brave the high rivers in a raft — you can even participate in the yearly raft races during the second weekend in June! If you're planning a tamer vacation, go hiking, rock hunting or fishing in the Rio Grande across the road, or in the many mountain lakes nearby. In the fall, come hunt in some of the finest elk and deer country in the Rocky Mountains!

Location: Off of Highway 149, near milepost 11-12.

13 housekeeping cabins
8 lodge rooms
15 dorm beds
2 trailers for rent
Camping available
Rates: $$ to $$$$

Bill & Thressia Philbern
Star Rt. 81133 (CB)
South Fork CO 81154
(719) 658-2479
(800) 326-6408

Pets: Yes
Elevation: 8,735
Credit Cards: No
Open all year

Chinook Lodge & Smokehouse

Nestled among tall pine trees, Chinook Lodge offers one- and two-bedroom log cabins with kitchens and native rock fireplaces. A small store sells groceries, snacks and hunting and fishing licenses. To whet your appetite, the smokehouse makes great hickory-smoked ham, turkey, fish and old-fashioned beef jerky.

This is a great area for fishing, hunting and skiing. Fish in the nearby gold-medal waters of the Rio Grande and many mountain lakes. The Rio Grand also provides fun whitewater rafting opportunities during the milder weather. In the winter, visit the cross-country and downhill ski areas close by.

Location: At the east edge of South Fork on Highway 160, near milepost 186.

8 housekeeping cabins
1 non-housekeeping cabin
Camping available
Rates: $$

Roy & Barb Pruett
29666 Highway 160 W
P.O. Box 530 (CB)
South Fork CO 81154-0530
(719) 873-9993
(800) 238-6837

Pets: Yes
Elevation: 8,400
Credit Cards: VMAD
Open all year

Cottonwood Cove Lodge, Cabins and Restaurant

Surrounded by thousands of acres of untouched mountains and nestled near the clear, icy waters of the Rio Grande, these cabins have one to three bedrooms, fireplaces, linens and kitchens with supplies. Choose either lodge rooms, cabins or dormitory beds. The lodge, built in 1946, has a cozy family room, a cafe featuring homemade pies, a recreational room, a children's playground, laundromat and a gift shop.

Advanced reservations are required for horseback rides.

Cottonwood Cove provides excursions on horseback or by four-wheel drive to nearby scenic areas. You're sure to catch many gold-medal fish in the Rio Grande and in nearby mountain lakes. Cross-country skiers, snowmobilers and mountain bikers will delight in the close proximity of the Wolf Creek Ski Area and hundreds of miles of surrounding National Forest roads.

Location: On Highway 149, near milepost 13.

24 housekeeping cabins
6 lodge rooms
32 dormitory beds
Camping available
Rates: $$ to $$$$$

Richard & Kathi Small
HC 33, Wagon Wheel Gap (CB)
South Fork CO 81154
(719) 658-2242

Pets: Yes (additional fee)
Elevation: 8,448
Credit Cards: No
Open May 1 to November 1

Rainbow Lodge & RV Park

The Rainbow Lodge features a variety of modern log housekeeping cabins and motel rooms for your stay in South Fork. All have fully equipped kitchens, color televisions with cable (HBO) and phones. Most have fireplaces and log walls. The smaller cabins include bunk beds, while the large ones sleep up to six people comfortably. Your kids will enjoy playing on the large lawn.

When making reservations, specify room size and whether you'd like a fireplace.

The lodge is within walking distance to the Rio Grande, which is great for beginning rafting and fishing. You can drive to the numerous, easily accessible mountain lakes in the vicinity.

Location: At the junction of Highway 160 and Highway 149.

16 housekeeping cabins
13 motel rooms without kitchenettes
Camping available
Rates: $$ to $$$$

Teri & Robert Byrd
P.O. Box 224 (CB)
South Fork CO 81154-0224
(719) 873-5571

Pets: Yes
Elevation: 8250
Credit Cards: VMAD
Open all year

Riverbend Resort Cabins & RV Park

In a mountain setting on the South Fork of the Rio Grande, Riverbend has a ¾ -mile riverfront of modern, well-heated cabins with fully equipped kitchens. If you have a large group, ask for accommodations in the triplex bunkhouse. Most rooms have fireplaces, while all have bed and bath linens, color television and a view of the river. Relax in the hot tub year round after a long day of hiking or skiing.

Fish on the private river or on the many lakes nearby. The riverbend is in the heart of Wolf Creek, which offers great hiking, exploring, hunting and snowmobiling. Be sure to check out the cross-country and downhill skiing at Wolf Creek Ski Area, which has the most snowfall of any ski area in Colorado.

Location: 3 miles southwest of South Fork on Highway 160, near milepost 183.

9 housekeeping cabins
18 bunkhouse or dorm beds
Camping available
Rates: $$ to $$$$$

Ralph & Cassie Laubersheimer
33846 West Highway 160
P.O. Box 129 (CB)
South Fork CO 81154-0129
(719) 873-5344

Pets: Yes
Elevation: 8,300
Credit Cards: VM
Open all year

Spruce Lodge, Rafting & RV Park

If you're into whitewater rafting, this is the place to stay. Built in the 1920s, this lodge is a quaint, historic accommodation that blends modern conveniences while retaining turn-of-the-century charm. Choose between comfortable bed and breakfast rooms or motel rooms, with or without a fully equipped kitchenette or television. If you don't want to cook your own meals, the dining room serves home-cooked, family style eats. After a full day of rafting, soothe your tired muscles in the spacious hot tub. You'll be fully entertained in the game room, which features a pool table, video games and a juke box. Outside, play miniature golf right on the premises.

Ask your hosts about rafting on the Rio Grande — there are mild, safe, fun family trips for novices. Enjoy the other area activities: trout fishing, snowmobiling, hunting and four-wheel drive trips. In the winter, reserve mountain sleigh rides, ice skate or ski at Wolf Creek Ski Area.

Location: North side of Highway 160, at the east end of South Fork, near milepost 187.

1 motel room with kitchenette
7 motel rooms without kitchenette
8 lodge or bed and breakfast rooms
10 bunkhouse or dorm rooms
Camping available
Rates: $$ to $$$

Dirk & Kileen Squibb
29431 Highway 160
P.O. Box 156 (CB)
South Fork CO 81154-0181
(719) 873-5605
(800) 228-5605

Pets: No
Elevation: 8,400
Credit Cards: VM
Open all year

STEAMBOAT SPRINGS AREA

Includes Clark and Hahn's Peak. Map: C-9

Famous as a Colorado ski center, Steamboat Springs offers much more to the tourists who frequent the Yampa Valley. Mountain biking, fishing, horseback riding and hiking are all ingredients for summer fun. The town of Steamboat Springs is an eclectic mix of the old and the new. Old-time Western-wear stores share sidewalk space with ice cream stores and T-shirt shops. For relaxation, you can choose from among the more than 150 hot springs in the Steamboat area. The northern Ute Indians were known to have summered in the area as early as the 1300s. According to Ute Indian legend, you must beware of the "Yampa Valley Curse": visitors to the valley are cast under a spell that compels them to return again and again.

Fun Things to Do

- Hahn's Peak Area Historical Society, Summer: (303) 879-3825; Winter: (303) 824-5176
- Hahn's Peak Schoolhouse (303) 879-6781
- Sheraton Steamboat Golf Course (303) 879-2220
- Steamboat Springs Golf Course (303) 879-4295
- Steamboat Springs Health & Recreation Association (303) 879-1828
- Strawberry Park Hot Springs (303) 879-0342
- Tread of Pioneers Museum (303) 879-2214

Elk River Guest Ranch

On the upper Elk River, surrounded by Routt National Forest and near the Mount Zirkel Wilderness area, this is an excellent place to get away from it all. Stay in the quaint, comfortable cabins, unwind in the hot tub and join your hosts around the nightly summer camp fires.

Feel free to bring your horse to stay in the corral.

As an outfitting service, Elk River Guest Ranch will prepare you for hunting or fishing on Steamboat and Pearl Lakes or on the more than 100 mountain lakes and 900 miles of streams nearby. The ranch also offers horseback rides of varying lengths, including lunch, to Pearl Lake. In the winter, try cross-country skiing or snowmobiling on 25 miles of groomed trails or downhill ski in Steamboat Springs. The outstanding scenery in the Elk River Valley is breathtaking all year long. Bring your camera to capture wildlife, wild flowers, rushing rivers and, in the fall, the aspen in their golden glory.

Location: 20 miles north of Steamboat Springs, on County Road 129, then turn right (east) on County Road 64 and go 3 miles.

4 housekeeping cabins
Camping available
Rates: $$$$$ to $$$$$$

Pat & Joey Barrett
29840 County Rd. 64 (CB)
Clark CO 80428
(303) 879-6220
(800) 750-6220

Pets: No
Elevation: 7,600
Credit Cards: VM
Open all year

Glen Eden Resort

Located in the heart of ranch and recreation country, Glen Eden has "contemporustic" duplexes on the Elk River, combining natural, rustic materials with contemporary interior design. All accommodations are completely furnished, from firewood to forks. All have mossrock fireplaces, two bathrooms, two bedrooms, a kitchen, sun porch and views of Mount Zirkel and Sand Mountain. The log-styled cedar lodge has a dining room, a bar and a conference room. For those nippier days, swim in the heated pool or soak in one of two hot tubs.

Kids under 12 stay free.

There are many activities available at the resort itself — tennis, mountain biking and private trout fishing on the Elk River and in high-country lakes. Your hosts can arrange horseback hunting trips to take advantage of Colorado's largest elk populations minutes away. You can also go horseback riding around the grounds and boating on nearby Steamboat Lake. The Mount Zirkel Wilderness area, 6 miles down the road, is perfect for summer hiking and winter cross-country skiing. For those less active, picnic in historical Hahn's Peak or ask your hosts about the many sightseeing opportunities.

Location: Near Hahn's Peak on County Road 129, near milepost 17.

27 housekeeping duplexes
Rates: $$$$$

Rich Landon
54737 Routt County Rd. 129
P.O. Box 908 (CB)
Clark CO 80428-0908
(303) 879-3907
(800) 882-0854

Pets: No
Elevation: 7,100
Credit Cards: VM
Open all year

Hahn's Peak Guest Ranch

At the foot of Hahn's Peak, Hahn's Peak Guest Ranch has four new, completely furnished log housekeeping cabins that sleep up to eight people. Each cabin has a kitchen, a full bathroom with a shower-tub and a hot tub for soaking after a full day of outdoor activities. The general store is well-stocked with groceries, hunting and fishing licenses, tackle, gifts and a little bit of "this and that." You'll love the home-cooking in the rustic restaurant — don't miss those home-baked pies and cinnamon rolls!

Fish to your heart's content on the three large lakes or miles of Brooks and streams. The ranch offers guided horseback trips up Hahn's Peak for breathtaking views. You can opt to ride your mountain bike or hike on the nearby trails during the milder months, while in the winter, take Routt County's best snowmobiling and snowmobile tours.

Location: 24 miles north of Steamboat Springs on County Road 129, near milepost 24.

4 housekeeping cabins
4 non-housekeeping cabins
Rates: $$$$

Mark Glorioso
60880 R.C.R. 129
P.O. Box 688 (CB)
Clark CO 80428-0688
(303) 879-5878
(303) 879-8638

Pets: No
Elevation: 8,300
Credit Cards: VM
Open all year

Inn at Steamboat Lake

This inn, a unique country-style bed and breakfast accommodation, is loaded with friendly hospitality. Each room, furnished with American country classics, contains a private bath and has a spectacular view from its private porch. The dining room is tastefully decorated and serves fine home-style food during regular hours. In the evening, gaze at the stars from the private hot tub. Visit the fishing tackle store for advice about local lake and stream fishing. All in all, this inn is the in a perfect setting for business retreats, seminars, weddings and family reunions.

The marina at Steamboat Lake offers everything from canoe and powerboat rentals to water skiing, sailing and wind surfing instruction. Hiking trails head into the million-acre Routt National Forest. Wranglers will take you for hourly, half-day, or full-day horseback rides to secluded areas on mountain trails. In the winter, rent one of the inn's snowmobiles or ski into the wilderness on cross-country ski trails.

Location: Located in the village of Hahn's Peak, 25 miles north of Steamboat Springs, on County Road 129, near milepost 24.

8 bed and breakfast lodge rooms
Rates: $$$$$

Tim Leonard
P.O. Box 839 (CB)
Clark CO 80428-0839
(303) 879-3906
(800) 934-STAY

Pets: No
Elevation: 8,100
Credit Cards: VMD
Open all year

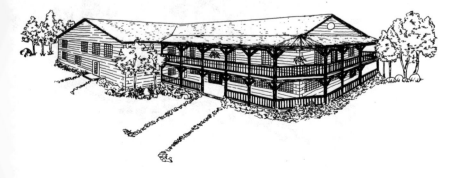

Perry-Mansfield Log Lodges

You'll find these modern log cabins in secluded and wooded Strawberry Park, one of the more beautiful areas in the region. These snug cabins, which sleep up to 10 people, contain electric baseboard heat, wood-burning fireplaces, full kitchens and bathrooms, including all linens and firewood. The rustic conference facility is ideal for business meetings and family reunions.

Perry-Mansfield, the oldest performing arts camp in the country, was a focal point for American modern dance in the 1930s. The performing arts tradition continues — in the summer, be sure to attend their lovely theater and dance productions. The area is ripe for hiking, fishing or swimming in the nearby hot springs pool. In the winter, you'll enjoy snowshoeing, cross-country skiing, sledding and downhill skiing at Steamboat Springs.

Location: In Steamboat Springs, go north on 7th from Lincoln, turn right on Missouri and continue to North Park. Follow North Park for 1½ miles. Perry-Mansfield is on the left.

6 housekeeping cabins
40 bunkhouse or dorm beds
Rates: $$$$$

Randy & Nina Cochran
40755 Routt County Rd. 36 (CB)
Steamboat Springs CO 80487-9298
(303) 879-1060

Pets: Yes
Elevation: 7,000
Credit Cards: VMA
Open all year

Steamboat Springs KOA & Cabins

Enjoy camping on the beautiful Yampa River in this KOA, which has both full housekeeping cabins and camper cabins. The campground has a heated pool, a hot tub, a miniature golf course, a game room, a children's playground, a small store and a laundromat.

From the property, go fishing and tubing in the Yampa River. You'll be near to the ski area, hunting, hot air ballooning, summer rodeo events, gondola rides and golfing. Take the city bus to Steamboat Springs shopping and entertainment. Don't pass up the natural hot springs, hiking and mountain biking trails in Steamboat Lake State Park. Steamboat Springs is conveniently located between Yellowstone and Rocky Mountain National Parks.

Location: Off of Highway 40, near milepost 129.

3 camper cabins
5 housekeeping cabins
Camping available
Rates: $$ to $$$$

Michael & Turid Sabia
29135 West Highway 40 (CB)
Steamboat Springs CO 80487
(303) 879-0273

Pets: Yes
Elevation: 6,800
Credit Cards: VM
Open all year

Stoner: see Dolores.

STONEWALL

Map: P-16

Stonewall, 30 miles west of Trinidad, is a small unincorporated town on the banks of the Purgatoire River. The "stone wall" is a dramatic, vertical wall of sandstone, a particularly striking occurrence of the Dakota Hogback formation that runs the length of Colorado. Listen to the gentle breezes while fishing and relaxing here — sure to soothe body and soul. For a touch of civilization, return to Trinidad, where there is a golf course and many interesting museums.

Fun Things to Do

- A.R. Mitchell Memorial Museum of Western Art (719) 846-4224
- Aultman Museum of Photography (719) 846-3881
- Baca House, Bloom House, Pioneer Museum (719) 846-7217
- Louden-Henritze Archaeology Museum (719) 846-5543
- Old Firehouse #1 Children's Museum (719) 846-7721
- Trinidad Golf Course (719) 846-4015

Stonewall Guest Ranch Cabins & RV Park

Travel the "Scenic Highway of Legends." Located on the Purgatoire River, at the base of the majestic Stonewall formation, this ranch has two- and three-bedroom cabins with carpeting, fireplaces and kitchens. Groups love the eight-bedroom historic lodge with its large, comfortable living room, country kitchen and a wonderful sunroom. Furnished with antiques and collectibles, it's like going to Granny's. There is a playground for kids, plus volleyball, basketball and a trout pond for people of all ages.

The Cuchara Valley Ski Resort is only 17 miles away, with slopes from beginner to expert. Take four-wheel drive roads or highway drives for some of the most beautiful mountain scenery. Fish in the Purgatoire and Cucharas Rivers and in nearby North Lake and Monument Lake. If you feel like traveling a bit, you might want to try a one-day jaunts to Taos, New Mexico or to Fort Garland and the Great Sand Dunes. In season, hunt for deer, elk, turkey, and bear in the San Isabel National Forest. All in all, this is a great place to relax in "God's Country."

Location: 29 miles west of Trinidad on Highway 12, near milepost 38.

3 housekeeping cabins
1 historic lodge group facility
Camping available
Rates: $$$ to $$$$

Darrell & Mary Fleming
6878 Highway 12 W (CB)
Weston CO 81091
(719) 868-2270
Groups: (806) 355-6008

Pets: Yes (in some units)
Elevation: 7,870
Credit Cards: No
Open all year

Strasburg: see Denver. Map: F-19

SUMMIT COUNTY

Includes Breckenridge, Dillon, Frisco, Green Mountain Reservoir,
Keystone and Silverthorne. Map: F-12.

Summit County offers year-round recreation, from outstanding ski areas to miles of summer hiking and biking trails. Go sailing on Lake Dillon or take a horse-drawn buggy ride through historic Breckenridge to see its numerous Victorian-style buildings. Shop in more than 50 Silverthorne Factory Outlet Stores or rent a mountain bike in Frisco and enjoy the trails of Summit County. Come in the winter to ski the slopes at Breckenridge, Keystone and Copper Mountain. You'll appreciate the warmth and charm of these unique mountain communities from January to December.

Fun Things to Do

- Breckenridge Golf Course (303) 453-9104
- Breckenridge Mining Camp Museum (303) 453-2342
- Copper Creek Golf Course, Copper Mountain (303) 968-2339
- Eagles Nest Golf Course, Silverthorne (303) 468-0681
- Frisco Historical Society Museum & Historic Park (303) 668-3428
- Keystone Ranch Golf Course, Keystone (303) 468-4250
- South Park Historical City Museum, Fairplay (719) 836-2387
- Summit Historical Society & Museum, Dillon (303) 453-9022
- Summit Historical Society, Breckenridge (303) 668-5800

Alpen Hütte Lodge

This beautiful lodge on the Blue River, at the foot of the Continental Divide, is styled after European mountain lodges. They offer clean, comfortable rooms that sleep up to eight people. Most rooms have bunks; however, if you prefer, ask for a queen-sized bed. This lodge is ideal for groups, retreats and reunions — you can eat meals economically in the winter or make them yourself in the kitchen facilities during the summer. Don't worry about noise; the lodge enforces a curfew to ensure a good night's sleep.

The lodge has facilities for the handicapped.

The Alpen Hütte is right on the Summit County Bike Path System, featuring over 50 miles of paved roads. Those who want more adventurous rides can rent one of the Trek mountain bikes to head up into the mountain highlands for unsurpassed mountain views. Hiking trails wind through towering evergreens, along majestic mountains, rivers and mountain lakes. Fish in gold-medal waters a few steps from your back door, or venture into the Eagle's Nest Wilderness. In the winter, ski on the many downhill ski areas nearby, including Arapahoe Basin, Keystone, Copper Mountain, Breckenridge, Vail and Loveland. Or you can cross-country ski on groomed trails at Nordic centers and in the wilderness areas.

Location: In Silverthorne.

11 lodge rooms
Rates: $ to $$ (per person)

Fran & Dave Colson
471 Rainbow Drive
P.O. Box 919 (CB)
Silverthorne CO 80498-0919
(303) 468-6336

Pets: No
Elevation: 8,500
Credit Cards: VMD
Open all year

Frisco Lodge

The oldest ongoing lodging facility in Summit County, the Frisco Lodge, built in 1885, served as a stagecoach stop and a railroad hotel. Eight European-style historic rooms share a large living room and three baths. The 10 modern suites have private baths. The lodge serves a delicious continental breakfast daily. Soak in the outdoor hot tub that overlooks the garden or take a workshop for maintaining your bicycle or tuning your skis.

In the summer, Summit County offers some of the best cycling in the country. Scenic road-bike trails reach Frisco from Copper Mountain, Keystone, Breckenridge, Dillon and Vail. There are plenty of mountain bike rides as well, both on Jeep and single track roads. Take a break and fish for trout and Kokanee salmon. In the winter, enjoy downhill skiing, visit the Nordic centers for groomed cross-country ski trails, or explore the backcountry skiing of the Gore Range Wilderness area.

Location: Main Street, downtown Frisco.

8 historic lodge rooms
10 motel rooms without kitchenette
Rates: $$ to $$$$$

Susan Wentworth & Bruce Knoepfel
321 Main St.
P.O. Box 1325 (CB)
Frisco CO 80443-1325
(303) 668-0195
(800) 279-6000

Pets: No
Elevation: 9,100
Credit Cards: VMAD
Open all year

Green Mountain Cabins & Boat Rentals

These light housekeeping cabins are in a beautiful location on the Green Mountain Reservoir, nestled between the Gore and Williams Fork Mountain Ranges.

The marina rents 14-foot fishing boats and canoes by the hour or by the day. Hike and watch the birds on the several nearby trail in the Eagle's Nest Wilderness area, with its pristine lakes and streams teeming with Brook trout. For the more adventurous, this area is great for windsurfing, hang gliding, waterskiing and backpacking.

Location: 17.3 miles north of the I-70 Silverthorne exit (exit 205), on Highway 9, near milepost 126. Turn west at the north end of the reservoir on South County Road 30 to Heeney.

3 housekeeping cabins
Rates: $$

Dick & Maggie Philips
0255 County Rd. 1782 Blue River Route
P.O. Box 82A (CB)
Heeney CO 80498-0082
(303) 724-9449
(303) 724-9748

Pets: Yes
Elevation: 8,500
Credit Cards: VM
Open all year

Green Mountain Inn

These old-style mountain cabins are ideal for your vacation or weekend plans. Either let them do the cooking — their restaurant prepares wonderful meals and fresh, homemade pies — or, for those with a gourmet flair, purchase supplies at the grocery store and cook your own on your cabin stove. Then join the tavern crowd for relaxing in this small, peaceful mountain town.

Green Mountain Reservoir and surrounding wilderness areas offer many activities, including fishing, boating, waterskiing, windsurfing, hiking, hunting and hang gliding.

Location: Go 17.3 miles north of I-70 at Silverthorne (exit 205) on Highway 9. Near milepost 126, turn west at the north end of the reservoir and go 7.3 miles on South County Road 30 to Heeney.

2 housekeeping cabins
Rates: $$

Tom & Davelyn Forrest
7101 South County Rd. 30 (CB)
Heeney CO 80498
(303) 724-3812

Pets: Yes
Elevation: 8,000
Credit Cards: VM
Open all year

Paradox Lodge

If you crave peace and quiet where the air is always clean and fresh, this is the place. Paradox Lodge overlooks the Snake River and is surrounded by the Arapaho National Forest on a 37-acre secluded alpine location. The completely furnished deluxe cabins and lodge rooms have kitchens and sleep up to five. Watch the clear, bright night stars from the wood-fired, community hot tub. All accommodations include breakfast to start your day right.

You can hike or cross-country ski right from your cabin door, or traverse the mountain bike and four-wheel drive trails. Paradox Lodge is just a few miles from Keystone and many Summit County ski areas. In Montezuma Valley, explore the historic mining district, including the many old gold and silver mines and ghost town sites. Summer brings a profusion of wildflowers, wildlife and music and balloon festivals, among other activities, into the area.

Location: Between Keystone and Montezuma on Montezuma Road (County Road 5) 5 miles east of Keystone, 13 miles from I-70 exit 205.

3 housekeeping cabins
4 lodge rooms
Rates: $$$$ to $$$$$

George & Connie O'Bleness
35 Montezuma Rd. (CB)
Dillon CO 80435
(303) 468-9445

Pets: Yes (cabins only)
Elevation: 10,050
Credit Cards: VMAD
Open all year

Tiger Run Resort

Nestled at the scenic fork of the Blue and Swan Rivers, Tiger Run has fully furnished and modern chalets that feature landscaped yards, cable television, patios, paved roads and parking. There is a luxurious clubhouse with an indoor pool, a hot tub, a game room, a laundromat facility and a convenience store. Play tennis or fish for trout on the streams and private lake right on the grounds. For RV enthusiasts, you can rent one of 125 paved sites by the night, week, or month. These sites have full hookups and cable television. If you're bringing a large group, you can meet in the large indoor/outdoor facility.

During the summer, you can take four-wheel drives, sail on Lake Dillon, river-raft, hike, horseback ride, bike, fish, golf or go ballooning. Winter brings dog-sledding, skiing at Breckenridge and Vail, ice skating, snowmobiling, sleigh riding, ice fishing and relaxing by the indoor heated pool. There is shopping and fine dining in nearby Breckenridge. The communities of Frisco, Keystone and Copper Mountain are also within a short drive for a variety of recreational and cultural opportunities.

Location: 3 miles north of Breckenridge on Highway 9.

16 mountain chalets
Rates: Call for prices

Russell, Jack, & Jeannette Whitt, Owners
Steve & Debbie Roderick, Managers
85 Tiger Run Rd. (County Road 315)
P.O. Box 815 (CB)
Breckenridge CO 80424-0815
(303) 453-9690

Pets: Yes
Elevation: 9,300
Credit Cards: VM
Open all year

Woods Inn International

Built of pine logs in 1938, this unique bed and breakfast inn, situated in the heart of Summit County, offers a variety of bedrooms decorated with a homespun flair. There are three sitting rooms and a spacious outdoor deck with an all-season spa. Enjoy a complimentary gourmet breakfast to start your day.

The surrounding lakes, rivers and mountain peaks provide you with year-round activities, from hiking and mountain biking to skiing and snowshoeing.

Location: 205 South 2nd Avenue in Frisco.

7 lodge rooms
Rates: $$ to $$$$$

Murray & Sue Bain
205 S. 2nd Ave.
P.O. Box 1302 (CB)
Frisco CO 80443-1302
(303) 668-3389

Pets: No
Elevation: 9,000
Credit Cards: VM
Open all year

Tarryall Reservoir: see Lake George. Map: H-14

Trinidad: see Stonewall. Map: P-19

TWIN LAKES

Includes Granite. Also see Leadville. Map: H-11

Twin Lakes, located at the base of Independence Pass, are natural, glacier-made lakes, measuring 90 feet deep, almost 2 miles wide and 6 miles long. You can fish from the shoreline or from a boat. The majestic mountain backdrop makes this area a photographer's dream.

Fun Things To Do

- Twin Lakes Nordic Inn Restaurant (800) 626-7812, (719) 486-1830

Callies Cabins & Twin Lakes Expeditions

These clean, cozy cabins are located at the base of Mount Elbert, Colorado's highest mountain, in scenic Twin Lakes. The newly renovated, comfortable cabins have rustic decor, yet include a private bath, individual heating and spectacular views. Join with other guests to play volleyball and horseshoes on the grounds.

Kids under 12 stay free.

Callies Cabins & Twin Lakes Expeditions offers a 10% discount on the nation's best whitewater rafting trips — and they provide front-door transportation, too!

Location: Highway 82, near milepost 79.

4 housekeeping cabins
Rates: $$$

Rick & Elaena Covington
6495 Highway 82
P.O. Box 70 (CB)
Twin Lakes CO 81251-0070
(719) 486-3928
(800) 288-0497

Pets: No
Elevation: 9,200
Credit Cards: VM
Open May 15 to October 31

Mount Elbert Lodge & Cabins

This is your home for year-round fun in the Colorado Rockies. On a river at the base of Mt. Elbert, this lodge is easily accessible, yet remotely private. The comfortable, rustic housekeeping cabins feature separate kitchen and living spaces, private bathrooms, baths and porches that encourage relaxing in the sun. The bed and breakfast lodge has six rooms, including the "Mount Elbert" room, with a southern exposure, private balcony and brass bed; and the "Mount Massive" room, with a view of the valley from its north and south windows. The lodge's common area has a fireplace for cozy winter retreats.

The lodge serves healthy and wholesome complimentary breakfasts. If you're hankering for a homemade dinner, make advance arrangements.

Hike, ski and snowmobile from your back door. The lodge forms a trailhead to Mount Elbert or you can climb several other "fourteeners" nearby. Enjoy the downhill skiing, excellent lake and stream fishing and some of the country's best whitewater rafting.

Location: Off of Highway 82, near milepost 74½. Approximately 4½ miles west of Twin Lakes.

6 housekeeping cabins
6 bed and breakfast rooms
Rates: $$$ to $$$$

Salina & Karl Martin
P.O. Box 40 (CB)
Twin Lakes CO 81251-0040
(719) 486-0594

Pets: Yes (extra fee; with restrictions)
Elevation: 9,800
Credit Cards: VM
Open all year (cabins have no running water in winter)

Olsen's Cabins & Store

Near the shore of the Twin Lakes, each of these six unique, modern cabins has its own bath facilities. All but one have kitchens. There is a nice fishing tackle and bait store on the premises, where you can get everything you need — including good advice.

Check with your hosts about lake, stream and Arkansas River fishing and rafting trips or venture out on your own.

Location: Off of Highway 82, near milepost 79.

5 housekeeping cabins
1 non-housekeeping cabin
Rates: Call for prices

Ken & Catherine Olsen
6563 Highway 82
P.O. Box 96 (CB)
Twin Lakes CO 81251-0096
(719) 486-0228

Pets: No
Elevation: 9,200
Credit Cards: VM
Open May 1 to September 15

Twin Lakes Nordic Inn

An authentic century-old stagecoach stop and former brothel, the Twin Lakes Nordic Inn has been romantically restored with imported Austrian featherbeds and antiques. All of the rooms are different in style, in view and in architecture. Some have their own baths; others have shared baths. The inn's restaurant, open all day, specializes in authentic German cuisine and fireside dining. They also feature a video room with a film library for those evenings when you just want to stay put. Try the new outdoor hot tub for soaking after a day on the trail.

Ask your host to arrange helicopter skiing in the early spring, river rafting trips on the Arkansas in the summer and houseboats for fishing or exploring the ghost town of Interloken. In the heart of the Pike-San Isabel National Forest on the shore of Twin Lakes, the Twin Lakes Nordic Inn is an ideal base camp for cross-country and alpine skiing, fishing, hiking, hunting and windsurfing. Twice a year, be sure to attend the "Hookers Ball" — but only with an appropriate costume!

Location: In Twin Lakes, off of Highway 82, near milepost 79.

18 historic hotel bed and breakfast rooms
Rates: Call for prices

John Slater
6435 Highway 82
P.O. Box 410 (CB)
Twin Lakes CO 81251-0410
(719) 486-1830
(800) 626-7812

Pets: Yes
Elevation: 9,227
Credit Cards: VM
Open all year

Twin Peaks Cabins

These modern, log-sided cabins have a lovely view of the south side of upper Twin Lakes, including the major mountain peaks of the Sawatch Range. The gift shop features leather and fur items and southwestern gifts.

Bring your boat to take advantage of the good fishing in lakes and streams. Hiking trails begin within walking distance of the cabins and offer enough scenery to keep photographers busy for years! The cabins are ¼ mile west of Twin Lakes on the road to Independence Pass, the "high road" to Aspen.

Location: Off of Highway 82, near milepost 78.

3 housekeeping cabins
Rates: $$ to $$$$

Fred & Judy Woodcock
6889 Highway 82
P.O. Box 86 (CB)
Twin Lakes CO 81251
(719) 486-2667

Pets: Yes (small fee per pet)
Elevation: 9,200
Credit Cards: VMD
Open May 15 to October 31

Win-Mar Cabins

In an excellent, central location, these log cabins have fantastic views of the highest peaks in Colorado. In addition, they're cozy, modern and clean; with fully equipped kitchens.

Fish for weeks on Twin Lakes, Clear Creek Reservoir and in the Arkansas River. Ask your hosts about other mountain adventures, such as hiking, hunting, mountain climbing, whitewater raft trips and gold panning. In the winter, there's good ice fishing, cross-country and downhill skiing and snowmobiling. Just a few miles down the road, you'll see the historic town of Leadville, with its famous Opera House and other period buildings.

Location: At the intersection of Highways 24 and 82, near milepost 191.

11 housekeeping cabins
Rates: $$ to $$$$$

Rod & Dolores Rodaway
Twin Lakes Star Rt. (CB)
Granite CO 81228
(719) 486-0785

Pets: Yes (small pets only)
Elevation: 9,000
Credit Cards: VMD
Open all year

U. S. Air Force Academy: see Colorado Springs Area. Map: H-17

VALLECITO LAKE AREA

Includes Bayfield. Also see Durango. Map: O-6

Vallecito Lake, located 23 miles northwest of Durango, lies under the snow-capped peaks of the San Juan National Forest. This area is an angler's delight — fish for Rainbow trout, Kokanee salmon and Northern pike.

Fun Things To Do

- Five Branches Horse Rides and Boat Rentals (800) 582-9580, (303) 884-2582
- Lake Haven Burger Stop (303) 884-2517
- Silver Streams Restaurant (303) 884-2770

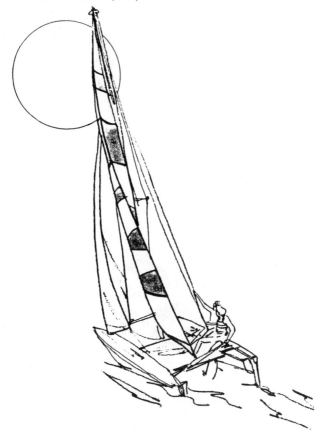

Bear Paw Lodge

When touring Southwest Colorado, Bear Paw Lodge is the place to stay. Its cabins, nestled among towering Ponderosa pines, blue spruce and aspen, each have a fireplace, full kitchen, barbecue facility and most have an outdoor picnic table. Some are on the creek or river.

Enjoy excellent springtime fishing and the reawakening of the valley. See spectacular colors in the fall while hunting deer and elk. Winter looks like a perpetual Christmas card in the Vallecito Valley. Enjoy cross-country skiing, tobogganing, ice skating, snowmobiling and sleigh rides. The lodge and cabins are within 1 mile of the marina on lake Vallecito, horseback riding stables, National Forest hiking trails, three restaurants and two country stores. Vallecito Lake has 22 miles of scenic shoreline and is bounded by National Forest and Wilderness areas. You'll be centrally located for all of the sights in the Durango area.

Location: Just northeast of Vallecito Lake.

12 housekeeping cabins
Rates: $$$$

Doug & Connie Allen
18011 County Rd. 501 (CB)
Bayfield CO 81122
(303) 884-2508

Pets: Yes
Elevation: 7,800
Credit Cards: VM
Open all year

Circle S Lodge

Journey to a high-country retreat in the beautiful San Juan Mountains, adjacent to the Weminuche Wilderness area on the north end of Vallecito Lake. Circle S Lodge features nicely decorated private mountain cabins that can accommodate up to nine people. Each completely carpeted cabin includes all linens, a fully equipped kitchen, a fireplace, an outdoor grill and a picnic table. For your convenience, they have a laundromat on the premises. The kids can have fun on the playground and fish in the small trout pond, while the adults can pitch horseshoes or play volleyball, badminton and basketball.

A 50% deposit of rental fee is required for reservations.

Adjacent to the San Juan Mountains and the Weminuche Wilderness, you'll want to rent horses and boats, fish in the lakes and rivers, hike and take pictures. Walk to the nearby grocery store and restaurant.

Location: Just northwest of Vallecito Lake.

7 housekeeping cabins
Rates: $$$$$

Steve & Cheryl Popely
18022 County Road 501 (CB)
Bayfield CO 81122
(303) 884-2473
(800) 658-8044

Pets: Yes (summer only)
Elevation: 7,850
Credit Cards: VMD
Open all year

Coolwater Ranch Cabins & Campground

The five cottage-style cabins are nestled beneath ancient pines beside the beautiful Pine River, also known as Los Piños Rio. Coolwater Ranch is quiet and off the highway, yet close to Vallecito Lake for restaurants and shopping. The cabins, equipped with kitchenettes, pots, pans, dishes and linens, offer modern comforts without modern hassles — no telephones or television, just a quiet country environment.

Check for special rates in May and September.

Enjoy trout fishing from your back door and in close by mountain streams, lakes and rivers.

Location: 2 miles south of Vallecito Lake.

5 housekeeping cabins/cottages
RV sites available
Rates: Call for prices

Thomas W. Beuten
10643 County Rd. 501 (CB)
Bayfield CO 81122-9701
(303) 884-2269

Pets: Yes
Elevation: 7,512
Credit Cards: No
Open May to September (weather permitting)

D'Mara Resort

Experience a touch of luxury in the wilderness in these spacious, secluded two- and three-bedroom vacation homes. On Grimes Creek by Vallecito Lake, these tastefully decorated cottages, with spectacular views of the majestic San Juan mountains, have modern kitchens with microwave ovens, fireplaces or wood stoves with free firewood, linens (provided and exchanged upon request) and outdoor barbecue grills. The vacation homes are accessible to the disabled.

Your hosts can reserve boat rentals on the lake and arrange rides on the Durango-Silverton Narrow Gauge Railroad or make dinner theater suggestions. Partake in the excellent fishing, skiing, horseback riding, hiking, bird watching, fine dining and, perhaps most importantly, peaceful relaxation.

Location: North of Vallecito Lake.

4 housekeeping cottages
Rates: $$$$$

Mara & David Edwards
1213 County Rd. 500 (CB)
Bayfield CO 81122
(303) 884-9806
(303) 884-9477

Pets: No
Elevation: 7,850
Credit Cards: No
Open all year

Elk Point Lodge

This nice resort on the quiet east shore of Vallecito Lake at Pine River features modern cabins with kitchens, tucked away into tall pines. All are either on the lakefront or with a lake view; some have fireplaces. The main lodge has a general store, a recreation room and a playground.

You can rent horses and boats on the property or fish the lake and Pine River. Elk Point Lodge is adjacent to the San Juan National Forest for horseback riding, mountain biking and hiking. With the Weminuche Wilderness only 3 miles away, your hosts can help plan your pack trips and expeditions for autumn elk, deer and small game hunting. Or just come to relax, watch a beautiful sunset from your porch and listen to the water gently lapping the shore.

Location: On Vallecito Lake's east shore. Follow paved road around west and north side of the lake. When the pavement ends, keep going south another 2 miles on dirt road.

9 housekeeping cabins
Rates: $$$ to $$$$$

Pete & Nancy Busby
21730 County Rd. 501 (CB)
Bayfield CO 81122-9703
(303) 884-2482

Pets: No (kennels available)
Elevation: 7,726
Credit Cards: VMA
Open May 1 to November 15

Lake Haven Resort

Whether you're planning an "on-the-go" or a "get-away-from-it-all" vacation, you'll love these cabins overlooking colorful Vallecito Lake. Built of local materials and situated among pines, the cabins have gas heat, dishes, linens and bedding, picnic tables and tubs or showers. Some have fireplaces; most have a lake view. An on-site store sells groceries, gifts, bait and tackle. This resort is ideal for small or large groups.

Make advance reservations to assure suitable accommodations. If you are flying in, send your arrival time so your hosts can arrange transportation from the airport.

Lake Vallecito offers many activities, from fishing and hunting to wilderness hiking and mountain biking. Photography buffs will find many subjects in beautiful lakes, streams, forested mountains and abundant wildlife.

Location: On the southwest shore of Vallecito Lake.

21 housekeeping cabins
Rates: $$ to $$$$$

J.D. & Fern Hudgpeth
14452 County Rd. 501 (CB)
Bayfield CO 81122-9701
(303) 884-2517

Pets: Yes (with restrictions)
Elevation: 7,500
Credit Cards: VM
Open May 1 to October 31

Pine River Lodge

These family owned and operated cabins, which overlook beautiful Vallecito Lake, have kitchens and feature aspen-, pine- or spruce-paneled walls. Some have fireplaces. The lodge has an indoor pool, a game room and a large playground.

There is excellent fishing in Vallecito Lake — anglers have set state records for Northern pike and Brown trout here. Hiking and horseback riding trailheads are all nearby. While visiting, be sure to take the Durango-Silverton Narrow Gauge Railroad and see the incredible Mesa Verde National Park. Also enjoy river rafting, melodrama, high stakes bingo and the Bar D Chuckwagon Diner. In the winter, you can snowmobile and ski close by.

Location: Overlooking Vallecito Lake's southwest shore.

24 housekeeping cottages
Rates: $$$ to $$$$

Donna, Debbie & Ermalee Atkinson
14443 County Rd. 501 (CB)
Bayfield CO 81122-9701
(303) 884-2563

Pets: Yes
Elevation: 7,800
Credit Cards: VM
Open all year

Silver Streams Lodge

At the north end of beautiful Vallecito Lake, you'll find modern housekeeping cabins with kitchen facilities and open-hearth fireplaces. Their family oriented restaurant serves breakfast, lunch, dinner and cocktails.

Cast your fishing rod into their private pond, stocked with Rainbow trout — no license or tackle required. Your host can arrange hunting and pack trips for a complete wilderness vacation. A lodge for all seasons, Silver Streams has wildflowers and fishing in the spring; boating, fishing and hiking in the summer; golden aspen and hunting in the fall; and cross-country skiing, snowmobiling and ice skating in the winter.

Location: At the north end of Vallecito Lake.

14 housekeeping cabins
Rates: $$$$

Jerry McCoy
18645 County Rd. 501 (CB)
Bayfield CO 81122-9703
(303) 884-2770

Pets: Yes
Elevation: 7,750
Credit Cards: VMD
Open all year

Vallecito Resort

There's something for everyone in the cool pines of Vallecito Resort. The 14 housekeeping cabins are equipped with linens, dishes and utensils. There's a small, private cabin for honeymooners and a large cabin suitable for family reunions. You'll find everything you need on site — a beauty salon, grocery store, two laundromats, recreation hall, cardroom, library and craft room.

Ask about off-season special rates.

Bring your square dance attire for evening dances: square (plus-C3), round (all phases), line and country swing. The resort sponsors many weekly activities, including Sunday church services, potlucks, poker, aerobics, bonfires, golf and bowling. Fish for state-record trout within walking distance. And don't forget to see the sights in the Durango area before you leave.

Location: Just south of Vallecito Lake.

10 housekeeping cabins
Camping available
Rates: Call for prices

Rex Hornbaker
13030 County Rd. 501 (CB)
Bayfield CO 81122
(303) 884-9458
Off-season: (303) 884-9782
(800) 258-9458

Pets: Yes
Elevation: 7,750
Credit Cards: VMD
Open May 1 to Oct 5

Wit's End Guest Ranch

Established in the 1860s, this ranch, which adjoins the 465,000-acre Weminuche Wilderness, was recently converted to guest facilities. Amid the dramatic setting, with 12,000- to 14,000-foot peaks on all sides, the cabins, some over 100 years old, have luxury furniture, stone fireplaces, kitchens, porch swings, queen-sized brass beds, all near streams, rivers and ponds. If you're planning a large group vacation, ask about the 7,000-square-foot cabin on the lake. The main lodge was the original barn — it's now furnished with a candle-lit restaurant, library, entertainment center and a dance floor. Listen to live music in the old-world bar, featuring mirrors from the 1836 Crystal Palace in London. Afterwards, soak in one of the four outdoor hot tubs or the large pool on the grounds. The Meadowlark Ranch, adjacent to Wit's End, has additional facilities for your convenience. Dine at all three restaurants during your stay. Be sure to pick up your vacation supplies and a few gifts at the general store.

Ask your hosts about the full American plan or the European plan when making your reservations.

Wit's End provides unlimited activities: carriage rides, fly fishing, moonlight cruises on the lake, mountain biking, tennis and swimming. They also arrange horseback rides, hayrides, rafting and wilderness trips.

Location: North of Vallecito Lake.

15 housekeeping cabins
6 housekeeping cabins at Meadowlark Ranch
Rates: $$$$$

Mary Ann Page, Manager
Jim & Lynn Custer, Owners
254 County Rd. 500 (CB)
Bayfield CO 81122-9702
(303) 884-9263
(303) 884-2110
Fax: (303) 884-4114

Pets: No
Elevation: 7,800
Credit Cards: VMD
Open all year

Wagon Wheel Gap: see South Fork and Creede. Map: N-9

Walden: see Gould. Map: B-12

Victor: see Cripple Creek. Map J-16

WESTCLIFFE

Map: L-15

When silver was king in 1881, the Denver & Rio Grande Railroad expanded from Cañon City into Westcliffe. Nearby Silver Cliff was legendary as one of the wild mining towns. You can explore these historical legends or go mountain biking, fishing and four-wheel driving by the colorful wildflowers.

Fun Things to Do

- Cross D Bar Trout Fishing (719) 783-2544, (719) 783-2227, Denver number: (303) 733-5577.
- Silver Cliff Museum (719) 783-2394
- St. Andrews/Westcliffe Golf Course (719) 783-2734

Alpine Lodge, Cabins & Dinner Restaurant

Bordering the San Isabel National Forest, these quaint mountain cabins are nestled among pine and aspen trees in the Sangre de Cristo Mountains. The cabins, which sleep up to four people in two bedrooms, have kitchens equipped with stoves, refrigerator's cooking utensils, and dishes. They also have private baths, with all towels and linens. Enjoy your evening meal in the restaurant, specializing in charbroiled steaks, seafood, sandwiches and delicious homemade soup and pies.

Over 100 miles of trails in the San Isabel National Forest await you for hiking and horseback riding during the summer and cross-country skiing in the winter. Start hiking on the trails from your cabin door to dozens of mountain streams and lakes. Or drive to Lake DeWeese for fishing, boating, or waterskiing. You can climb many of the nearby 13,000- to 14,000-foot peaks in a day without technical equipment — don't be surprised to see eagles flying high above you. Photograph the wildflowers, splashing color through the meadows and mountainsides. In the fall, hunt elk, antelope, deer, bear, mountain lion, Big Horn sheep and wild turkey.

Location: 10 miles southwest of Westcliffe on Highway 69, near milepost 55-56.

5 housekeeping cabins
Camping available nearby
Rates: $$

David Leugers
6848 County Rd. 140 (CB)
Westcliffe CO 81252
(719) 783-2660

Pets: No
Elevation: 9,000
Credit Cards: VM
Open all year

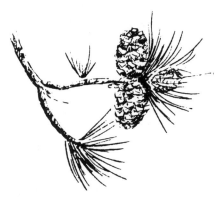

Weston: see Stonewall. Map: P-17

WINTER PARK

Map: E-14

Located in the beautiful Fraser Valley 67 miles west of Denver, Winter Park is home to numerous winter and summer activities. Winter finds snowmobiling and world-class skiing, while summer gives way to fishing, hiking, whitewater rafting and dazzling scenery. There is also a mountain bike trail system that will delight two-wheeler beginners or experts.

Fun Things to Do

- Pole Creek Golf Course (303) 726-8847
- Ski Train (303) 296-4754

Snow Mountain Ranch/YMCA of the Rockies

On 4,950 acres near Rocky Mountain National Park, Snow Mountain Ranch has large, private modern housekeeping cabins equipped with bedding, linens, towels, cooking utensils and dishes. The cabins include two to five bedrooms, while the lodge rooms sleep up to six people. All rooms have fireplaces. For your convenience, the ranch has a grocery store, restaurant, snack bar and library. They can accommodate groups of 1,500 people at their conference facilities — great for either a small seminar or huge family reunion. Stay on site to swim in the indoor pool, play tennis or roller skate in the skating rink.

When making reservations, request either the American or Modified American meal plans.

Snow Mountain Ranch sponsors many activities, such as family and youth programs, hiking, horseback rides and cross-country skiing. Bring your downhill skis for skiing at Winter Park and Silver Creek.

Location: Between Winter Park and Granby on Highway 40, near milepost 219.

40 housekeeping cabins
175 lodge rooms
Camping available
Rates: $$ to $$$$$

Kent Meyer
P.O. Box 169 (CB)
Winter Park CO 80482-0169
(303) 726-4628
Denver: (303) 443-4743

Pets: No
Elevation: 8,800
Credit Cards: No
Open all year

Wolcott: see Gypsum. Map: F-10

Woodland Park: see Colorado Springs Area. Map: I-17

YAMPA

Map: D-9

Yampa is located 30 miles south of Steamboat Springs, just west of the Routt National Forest. Fish and relax to your heart's content.

Fun Things to Do

- Bear River Recreation Area (303) 638-4516
- Finger Rock Rearing Unit (303) 638-4490
- Royal Egeria Theatre (303) 638-9986 or (303) 638-4463

Eagle Rock Lakes & Cabins

These modern lakeside housekeeping log cabins ensure you of a quiet and clean secluded spot to rest and enjoy trout fishing at its best — four private spring-fed trout lakes are located on 240 acres at the end of the road. As a guest, you have full privileges of the Eagle Rock Lakes and grounds.

Besides fishing on the lakes, you can fish in nearby creeks, reservoirs and the Yampa River. This area is also great for big-game hunting during the fall.

Location: 2 miles east of Yampa, off of Highway 131, near milepost 42, on County Road 8.

7 housekeeping cottages
Rates: $$$$$

Larry & Pauline Flanagan
29830 Routt County Rd. 8
P.O. Box 197(CB)
Yampa CO 80483-0197
(303) 638-4617

Pets: Yes
Elevation: 8,100
Credit Cards: No
Open May 14 to November 10

INDEX

NOTES

Tell your friends, so they can have their own copy
Check your local bookstore, or use this.

ORDER FORM

🏠 C O L O R A D O 🏠

CABINS
COTTAGES
& LODGES

Discover Scenic Vacation Hideaways

- From Modern to Rustic
- Close-in to Remote
- Friendly Places to Go
- Plus Local Fun Things to Do

TO ORDER, Phone toll-free, or mail this to:
Rocky Mountain Vacation Publishing, Inc.
5101 Pennsylvania Ave, Suite #5, Boulder, CO 80303-2799

Denver Area: **(303) 499-9385**
FAX: **(303) 499-9333**

(800) 886-9343

Cost per book	$12.95	$
Shipping and handling	$ 3.50	$
Colorado residents add 3.8% tax	$ .49	$
Total		$

Payment Method

☐ Check or money order is enclosed

Please bill credit card

☐ **VISA**® (13 or 16 digits)   ☐ **MasterCard**® (16 digits)

Expiration Date ☐☐ Month   ☐☐ Year

Credit Card # ☐☐☐☐☐☐☐☐☐☐☐☐☐☐☐☐

Signature _____

Name _____
U.P.S. Address _____

Tell your friends, so they can have their own copy
Check your local bookstore, or use this.

ORDER FORM

🏠 COLORADO 🏠

CABINS
COTTAGES
& LODGES

Discover Scenic Vacation Hideaways

- From Modern to Rustic
- Close-in to Remote
- Friendly Places to Go
- Plus Local Fun Things to Do

TO ORDER, Phone toll-free, or mail this to:
Rocky Mountain Vacation Publishing, Inc.
5101 Pennsylvania Ave, Suite #5, Boulder, CO 80303-2799

Denver Area: **(303) 499-9385**
FAX: **(303) 499-9333**

(800) 886-9343

Cost per book	$12.95	$
Shipping and handling	$ 3.50	$
Colorado residents add 3.8% tax	$ .49	$
Total		$

Payment Method

☐ Check or money order is enclosed

Please bill credit card

☐ **VISA** (13 or 16 digits)

☐ **MasterCard**® (16 digits)

Expiration Date ☐☐ ☐☐
Month   Year

Credit Card # ☐☐☐☐☐☐☐☐☐☐☐☐☐☐☐☐

Signature _____

Name _____

U.P.S. Address _____

ABOUT THE AUTHORS

Hilton and Jenny Fitt-Peaster are considered to be the foremost experts in Colorado on cabins, cottages and lodges. Since 1977, they have served as the executive directors of Colorado Association of Campgrounds, Cabins & Lodges. In 1980, they began publishing the annual *Colorado Directory of Cabins, Lodges, Camping, Fun Things To Do.* They became licensed real estate professionals in 1983 for the express purpose of brokering campgrounds, cabins and lodges — in 1985, they founded Colorado Campground Resort Realty, Inc., the only brokerage in Colorado that specifically sells cabin resorts, lodges and campgrounds statewide. In 1988, the authors founded the Colorado Cabin Resort Association, which merged with the Colorado Campground Association in 1991 to become the Colorado Association of Campgrounds, Cabins & Lodges of today.